Britain's Best Ever Political Cartoons

Tim Benson is Britain's leading authority on political cartoons. He runs the Political Cartoon Gallery and Café in Putney. He has produced numerous books on the history of cartoons, including *Giles's War*, *Churchill in Caricature*, *Low and the Dictators*, *The Cartoon Century: Modern Britain Through the Eyes of its Cartoonists*, *Drawing the Curtain: The Cold War in Cartoons*, *Over the Top: A Cartoon History of Australia at War* and *How to be British: A Cartoon Celebration*.

BRITAIN'S BEST EVER
POLITICAL CARTOONS

EDITED BY TIM BENSON

JOHN MURRAY

Dedicated to the memory of my parents Renee and Jack Benson

First published in Great Britain in 2021 by John Murray (Publishers)
An Hachette UK company

1

Cartoons copyright © Contributing cartoonists
Foreword copyright © Matthew Parris 2021
Introduction, captions and selection copyright © Tim Benson 2021

The right of Tim Benson to be identified as the Author of the Work has been asserted by him in accordance with the Copyright, Designs and Patents Act 1988.

Cartoons reproduced courtesy of Mirrorpix/Reach Licensing: pages 58, 68, 72, 76, 84, 89, 93, 108; Punch Cartoon Library/Topfoto: pages 62, 65, 77, 88, 100; Solo Syndication: pages 40, 53, 59, 61, 63, 69, 70, 73, 78, 80, 82, 87, 92, 94, 95, 98, 102, 104, 106, 107, 109, 112, 115, 121.

Book design by Janette Revill

A CIP catalogue record for this title is available from the British Library

Hardback ISBN 978-1-529-33439-5
eBook ISBN 978-1-529-33441-8

Typeset in Goudy Oldstyle

Printed and bound in Italy by L.E.G.O Spa

John Murray policy is to use papers that are natural, renewable and recyclable products and made from wood grown in sustainable forests. The logging and manufacturing processes are expected to conform to the environmental regulations of the country of origin.

John Murray (Publishers)
Carmelite House
50 Victoria Embankment
London EC4Y 0DZ

www.johnmurraypress.co.uk

FOREWORD BY MATTHEW PARRIS

Slowly but surely, the idea has crept up on our age that disrespect can never be justified. Civilised debate? Yes. Polite disagreement? Of course. Passionate advocacy? No problem. Even fierce disagreement is tolerated. But disrespect? Mere impertinence? Ridicule? No: we must never sneer, never 'gratuitously' offend.

Ridicule is going right out of fashion. Slated as 'disrespect' – which is now considered unforgiveable – it's under siege. Hate-speech legislators, no-platformers and the no-platformed compete with each other for the status of 'victim', the offended party. All sides display their wounds with lip-smacking relish . . . shrieking, 'You offended me!' 'No – *you* offended *me*!'

Everywhere, the citadels of the scornful are falling. We have 'lowered the tone', we have 'trivialised', we have 'resorted to playground insults'. And, out of step with our times, we slink away.

But not the political cartoonists. Almost alone now, almost an anachronism, they still stand, fearless and funny, farting in the face of all that is pompous and self-regarding in modern public life. Careless of the courtesies, blithely oblivious of the modern imperative to make a 'positive contribution' to the debate, our political cartoonists now wield almost the only pins left in the balloon factory that is politics.

How can I forget my nineteen-year-old self's shock and delight, arriving in the land of my forebears but not of my birth, to open a British newspaper for almost the first time and clap astonished eyes on a Scarfe cartoon of the newly victorious Margaret Thatcher as a poodle, excreting an elaborate turd composed of Edward Heath's face, and ending in a Mr Whippy-style flourish – his nose. Was that respectful? No. Constructive? Anything but. A positive contribution to the debate? Heaven forbid. Was it gratuitous? Oh, deliciously. Juvenile? Triumphantly. Offensive? You bet.

'So this is Britain!' I said to myself. And it was. Still is, I hope, in those precious little safe spaces for ridicule that our news media have ring-fenced off from the deadening culture of respect. Page on from these mere words to the feast of ridicule that follows, and know that there's still one redoubt for those of us for whom scorn and hilarity have a part to play in the po-faced parade that is twenty-first-century public affairs. As you'll see, our wonderful cartoonists mocked their way shamelessly through the eighteenth, nineteenth and twentieth centuries, and mock shamelessly on through the twenty-first.

And here's the irony. Ridicule *does* have a positive contribution to make to politics. If arrogance and vacuity are the disease, impertinence is the cure. Survey the world's more preposterous dictators and demagogues. What do they need? Not, I suggest, a 'constructive contribution to the debate'. That only dignifies them. Make fun of them instead. Here at home our own political masters are not monsters, but their calling invites high-handedness, self-aggrandisement, windbaggery and disingenuousness. They don't need platforms for debate: they just need to be taken down a peg or two – and the best way is to laugh at them. For centuries Britain's cartoonists have helped us do so, and this book is not least a tribute to mockery.

So never mind speaking truth to power, cock your leg to power, I say. Long may our cartoonists sprinkle ridicule on the turn-ups of the mighty. Read on!

INTRODUCTION

For almost three hundred years cartoonists in Britain have, with just sheets of paper or pieces of art board, pens or brushes and some Indian ink, produced images that have encapsulated the history of the United Kingdom.

No other medium, written or visual, has come quite as close to capturing the major events of the past as well as the political cartoon. This is all the more impressive when you consider that cartoonists, unlike historians, have to interpret events as they happen, rather than with either the benefit of hindsight or a proverbial crystal ball to hand. Margaret Thatcher, when prime minister, stated that the cartoon was 'the most concentrated and cogent form of comment . . . and the most memorable, giving the picture of events that remained most in the mind'. And the man she faced across the despatch box at the time, Michael Foot, leader of the Opposition and formerly editor of the *Evening Standard*

during the Second World War, completely agreed with her. He eloquently summed up the importance of political cartoons by stating that 'There is nothing to touch the glory of the great cartoonists. They catch the spirit of the age and then leave their own imprint upon it.' Politicians like Thatcher and Foot always enjoyed finding themselves in the cartoons of the daily newspapers, however disparaging or vilifying their portrayal, and appearing regularly in cartoons has always been a clear indication of a politician's importance. Winston Churchill noted that they need to worry when they stop appearing in them: 'Just as eels are supposed to get used to skinning, so politicians get used to being caricatured. In fact, by a strange trait in human nature they even get to like it. If we must confess it, they are quite offended and downcast when the cartoons stop.'

Over the centuries, political cartoonists in Britain have earned themselves an unsurpassed reputation for being the best in the world, a distinction that still holds true to this day. Yet not all of our great cartoonists were born and bred here. Will Dyson and David Low, two radical and innovative Antipodeans who would leave their own indelible imprint on British cartooning, had both already established themselves in Australia. However, they knew very well that in the early part of the twentieth century London's Fleet Street was the epicentre of newspaper journalism. After Dyson and Low moved to London and proved themselves successful, others followed: from America, Percy Fearon ('Poy'); from Hungary and Czechoslovakia, Victor Weisz ('Vicky') and Stephen Roth, both of whom had fled from the Nazis very shortly before the outbreak of the Second World War. After the war came Canadian Wally Fawkes ('Trog') and three New Zealanders, Neville Colvin, Les Gibbard and Nicholas Garland. There was also John Jensen from Sydney, the son of Australian cartoonist Jack Gibson. We still import the best talent from abroad, such as Americans Kevin Kallaugher and Rebecca Hendin, Peter Schrank from Switzerland and the Norwegian Morten Morland. These outsiders, with their own distinct perspective on our body politic,

have built upon and added to our rich cartoon heritage.

One of the most significant reasons why political cartoonists have flourished here is largely due to the country's long democratic traditions of free speech and tolerance of opinion. Over time these have allowed a free and inquisitive press to develop: as early as the beginning of the eighteenth century, London boasted the biggest, freest and most profitable newspapers in the world.

Just under a hundred years ago, when neither social media nor multi-channel 24/7 television existed and radio was still in its infancy, national newspaper circulation was in the millions. For the general public the papers were the only accessible means of finding out what was going on at home and abroad. Although the majority of journalists remained anonymous to their readers, cartoonists became well known either by their real names or the pseudonyms under which they worked. Readers might even know what the cartoonists looked like because some, such as Low and Vicky, had the audacity to depict themselves in their cartoons, observing events or even interacting with the leading politicians of the day. Their celebrity was acknowledged by the fact that until 1940, Madame Tussauds displayed waxworks of David Low, Percy Fearon and Sidney Strube. The exalted status of cartoonists – not to mention the huge discrepancy in salaries – led to a modicum of resentment from journalists. Having been one himself, Michael Foot believed that 'journalists are in, their heart of hearts, if they have such, deeply jealous. For the cartoonists, the truly great ones, achieve their effects by methods with which their fellow craftsmen cannot hope to compete.'

As cartoonists became highly valued within Fleet Street, the best of them received remuneration far exceeding that of journalists – or even editors. In 1931, for example, *Daily Express* cartoonist Sidney Strube had his salary doubled to £10,000 per annum both to match the earnings of sports cartoonist Tom Webster at the *Daily Mail* and to stop him being poached by the *Daily Herald* for the same money – at that time you could buy a house in central London for under £1,000. Other cartoonists since then have earned similarly high sums, demonstrating both their popularity and their importance to their respective newspapers.

Discounting cave paintings and illustrated pamphlets, it is generally accepted that visual satire began in the eighteenth century with the exceptional talent of William Hogarth. Although he did some engravings on political themes, he is better known for his social commentary through satirical prints and paintings. His most famous work is considered to be *Gin Lane*, an intricate etching that powerfully depicts London's urban poor struggling with the evils of gin addiction and which demonstrates both his wicked sense of humour and his heartfelt concern for his fellow Londoners.

Gin Lane proved a huge success for Hogarth, most notably because on its publication he became the first visual satirist to produce and sell prints, thereby increasing his popularity and reputation while also making himself a wealthy man.

Hogarth's entrepreneurial spirit directly paved the way for James Gillray, Britain's first professional political caricaturist. Gillray was a skilled engraver who took the novel step of accentuating the physical features of his political subjects and he was the first person to market his satirical prints in colour. He was aided and abetted by one of London's leading print sellers, Hannah Humphrey, whose shop window in St James's Street was always adorned with his latest prints; conveniently, Gillray lived above the shop. An observer at the time wrote of the impact when new Gillrays appeared in Humphrey's windows: 'The enthusiasm is indescribable when the next drawing appears. It is a veritable madness. You have to make your way through the crowd with your fists.'

Gillray spared no one, mercilessly ridiculing the leading political figures of the day, including William Pitt, Napoleon Bonaparte, the Prince of Wales and Charles James Fox. Surprisingly, in 1797 the government bought off Gillray with a pension, but his reputation survived and he became well known at the time as the 'Shakespeare of the etching needle'. The greatest political cartoonist of the twentieth century, Sir David Low, described Hogarth and Gillray respectively as the grandfather and father of the political cartoon.

By the 1840s, Gillray's vicious and explicitly disrespectful approach to political satire in individual prints had been replaced by cartoons generally found in respectable magazines and journals such as *Punch*, which was to monopolise visual satire in Britain for the rest of the nineteenth century and even spawned imitators in both Japan and Australia. There were briefly two rival satirical publications in Britain, namely *Fun* and *Tomahawk*, the former sometimes being characterised as a poor man's *Punch*. Even though *Fun* was seen as liberal in comparison with the increasingly conservative *Punch*, like *Tomahawk*, it folded within a few years.

It was John Leech in *Punch* (page 8) who first coined the term 'cartoon' for a satirical drawing, and it stuck. John Tenniel took over from Leech as lead cartoonist and became the pre-eminent practitioner of the art form throughout Queen Victoria's long reign. He was also the first cartoonist to be knighted for his work at *Punch*, as well as for his memorable illustrations for Lewis Carroll's *Alice's Adventures in Wonderland* and *Through the Looking-Glass*. When Tenniel retired in 1901 due to failing eyesight, *Punch* began its long, slow decline in readership and influence. Within the first few years of the twentieth century, it was struggling to compete with the new mass-market tabloid press.

Early on the tabloids started to employ political cartoonists to break up the visually monotonous pages of solid text – printers had not yet mastered photographic reproduction. Soon all the popular tabloids had regular political cartoons, unlike the broadsheets which, for many years, considered them far too frivolous. Today the situation has come full circle as political cartoons are only found regularly in serious broadsheets such as *The Times*, *Guardian*, *Independent* and *Daily Telegraph*. Sadly, not a single tabloid carries regular political cartoons any longer as they are, rather ironically, seen by their editors as too intellectually demanding for their readers.

The primary purpose of the political cartoon had originally been to support the editorial/political line of the newspaper, and to a certain extent that still holds true today. Cartoonists were expected to produce several ideas or sketches for the next day's cartoon, which would then be discussed with, and explained to, the editor. According to Carl Giles, formerly of the *Daily Express*, on the whole cartoonists would 'nervously approach the editor's office with a number of rough ideas and hope that at least one might meet with approval'. In this way, cartoons were unlikely to be out of tune with the paper's readership.

In September 1927, however, David Low agreed a contract with Lord Beaverbrook at the *Evening Standard* allowing him complete freedom in the selection and treatment of his subject matter. This was a first for a political cartoonist, though the paper reserved the right to refuse to publish. What made Low's position even more interesting was that his own political sympathies did not lie with those of the Tory-leaning paper he had just joined. His cartoons, therefore, often caused waves of protest when angry readers wrote to complain about Low ridiculing Conservative politicians. Of course, having opposing views in a single paper encouraged controversy, making it far more lively. When Low finally left the *Evening Standard* he joined the *Daily Herald*, which was more in sympathy with his own political beliefs, but he learned to his cost that preaching to the converted lessened the impact of his work.

Today, leading cartoonists such as Steve Bell, Morten Morland, Dave Brown and Peter Brookes have far greater freedom of expression than Low ever had. This is primarily because many of the sensitivities and taboos of the past have long since disappeared. What would have been considered indecent and in extremely bad taste seventy years ago is now perceived to be tame and inoffensive. Up until the 1960s, for example, royalty had to be treated with deference and the solemnity surrounding the death of a monarch might mean no cartoons at all would appear. None was published on the death of George V and only very staid and dignified ones on the deaths of Queen Victoria, Edward VII and George VI.

Unlike a newspaper article which can take a few minutes to read and digest, a good cartoon can be understood and appreciated immediately. The cartoonists will normally get most of their ideas for the next day's cartoon from that day's morning newspapers, or from radio, television, the internet or social media. However, unlike journalists who follow and report on the news, the cartoonists react to it; being reactive rather than proactive, cartoons consequently tend to appear negative. It is no surprise that *Guardian* cartoonist Steve Bell calls the cartoon 'art with attitude', while *Spitting Image* creator Roger Law refers to it as a naturally unfair art form.

This anthology contains cartoons that have both recorded and symbolised significant historical events at home and abroad over the past four centuries. Some have even created their own little bit of history and others have, over time, gained iconic status. Anyone who has studied history or politics will have noticed many of these outstanding cartoons in textbooks, journals, biographies and histories, and on websites. As a consequence, someone with an interest in history or politics who is asked to name a famous cartoon might easily describe not just one but several, though possibly be unable to give details of the captions, the artists or where they were published. The imagery and composition of, say, Gillray's 'Plum Pudding', Tenniel's 'Dropping the Pilot', Low's 'Rendezvous' or Zec's 'Here you are! Don't lose it again!' have become part of our common consciousness over the years. Nowhere else in the world has the political cartoon had such an impact on society as a whole. It is far easier to make a list of the greatest cartoons published in Britain than to name ten comparable ones from elsewhere. In America, besides Thomas Nast's 'Boss Tweed' or Bill Mauldin's cartoon of Lincoln with his head in his hands after the assassination of President Kennedy, the vast majority of American historians would struggle to name even one other, especially from the last seventy years.

If asked what makes a great political cartoon, I would say it is the synthesis of outstanding draughtsmanship and the ability to comment on an event or situation in a vivid, perceptive and imaginative way. This may be done either satirically or, for dramatic effect, poignantly. The composition is also essential for ease of interpretation and appreciation, while its dynamics can help heighten the impact. Michael Foot told me that the best cartoonists have 'finely tuned political antennae' and can regularly distil complex events into a simple visual metaphor so that the reader can instantly comprehend the political context behind it.

Political cartoonists have facilitated the memory of the great cartoon by a long-standing tradition of alluding to previous classics, with Sir John Tenniel's 'Dropping the Pilot' (page 16) the first example of a cartoon to be referenced by other editorial cartoonists. This practice is unique to the United Kingdom. It is only in the last sixty years that James Gillray's cartoons have become popular as allegories, largely as a result of a biography published in 1965 by American cartoonist Draper Hill. Gillray had long been dismissed as vulgar by the Victorians and consequently soon forgotten but, thanks to Hill, he is now held in the highest esteem. Apart from Gillray, it is probably David Low whose work is most frequently alluded to, as can be witnessed within the pages of this anthology. Nowadays, allegorical pastiches are more popular than ever, especially with cartoonists such as Steve Bell of the *Guardian* and Dave Brown of the *Independent*. The use of allusion and the words 'With apologies to . . .' or 'After . . .' help keep such classic works in the readers' minds and recognise the original cartoon's significance, with imitation being the sincerest form of flattery.

Frequently it is the controversy that a cartoon causes that makes it memorable, albeit not always for the reason intended by the cartoonist. Unlike the written word, a cartoon, as a visual image, can be easily misinterpreted and, on occasions, with serious repercussions –

with 'Price of petrol' (page 84), Zec was trying to advise the public to conserve fuel as wasting it was costing the lives of merchant seaman bringing it across the Atlantic, yet members of the wartime Cabinet saw it very differently.

Great cartoons tend to feature political leaders such as prime ministers, presidents and dictators. Cartoonists have it in their power to make them either heroes or villains depending on their own political convictions: Winston Churchill, for example, the most cartooned politician in British history, was portrayed as both during his decades-long career. Mercilessly ridiculed by cartoonists before the war for his political misjudgements, in 1940 they made him into a symbol of Britain's dogged defiance in the face of the Nazi onslaught. Sidney Strube said 'the political cartoonist is a powerful weapon for good or evil, and in a righteous cause should be used like a giant'. Such so-called giants in turn directly upset Napoleon, Kaiser Wilhelm II, Mussolini, Franco and Adolf Hitler. Napoleon constantly complained about Gillray, and Kaiser Wilhelm never forgave the cartoonists at *Punch* for their vitriolic treatment of him and looked forward to seeking retribution as soon as his armies had defeated Britain.

Throughout the 1930s, British cartoonists needled the Nazi leadership by ridiculing the Führer. During the Berlin Olympics Strube produced a cartoon to which Hitler himself took an instant dislike, resulting in the order being given that all copies of that day's *Daily Express* were to be confiscated on arrival in Germany. A year later, Foreign Secretary Lord Halifax held talks with Germany's Minister of Propaganda, Josef Goebbels, who complained that British cartoonists were damaging Anglo-German relations, singling out David Low for special attention. When he returned to England, Halifax informed the *Evening Standard*'s manager, Michael Wardell, who was asked to arrange a meeting between Halifax and Low: 'You cannot imagine the frenzy that these cartoons cause. As soon as a copy of the *Evening Standard* arrives, it is pounced upon for Low's cartoon, and if it is of Hitler, as it generally is, telephones buzz, tempers rise, fevers mount, and the whole governmental system of Germany is in uproar. It has hardly subsided before the next one arrives. We in England can't understand the violence of the reaction.' Halifax personally asked Low to modify his criticism of Hitler, to which Low agreed, although the respite lasted only three weeks; when Hitler invaded and occupied Austria, Low felt vindicated and consequently renewed his attack on the Nazi regime. The meeting between Low and Halifax is probably the only time a senior member of the Cabinet has censored a cartoonist. After the war, Low and the other Fleet Street cartoonists found their names on a Nazi death list.

Cartoonists have often got under the skin of British prime ministers too. Stanley Baldwin once called David Low 'evil and malicious', while Winston Churchill accused him of being 'a socialist of the Trotskyite variety'. Churchill was enraged by Zec's 'Price of petrol' cartoon and retaliated by trying to ban publication of the *Daily Mirror* and having Zec investigated by MI5. In his later years in office, Churchill was upset and hurt by Illingworth's *Punch* cartoon (page 100). His successor, Anthony Eden, complained daily to his Chief Whip Edward Heath over the treatment meted out to him during the Suez Crisis. John Major felt Steve Bell was trying to destabilise him by depicting him wearing underpants over his trousers, while a somewhat vain Tony Blair hated being portrayed with a receding hairline. Both Gordon Brown and David

Cameron complained at being illustrated as fat. Cameron also disliked Steve Bell's depiction of him wearing a prophylactic over his head, telling the cartoonist to his face that 'you can only push the condom so far'. This is not to say that all cartoonists were successful in undermining those in power. Vicky's parody of the doddery Edwardian Harold Macmillan as 'Supermac' backfired when the public failed to recognise the irony the cartoonist had intended. In fact, the Superman image actually enhanced the prime minister's standing so Vicky dropped it shortly afterwards.

In the past, symbolic figures were commonly used in editorial cartooning to represent either countries or their populace. In this anthology we can see how Raven-Hill used the popular symbol of America, Uncle Sam (page 39), while James Gillray and Bernard Partridge used John Bull to personify England (pages 4 and 50). Although clearly outdated, they are still recognised today as national symbols. Both the Zec cartoons have the heroic image of a British serviceman – in the guise of a merchant seaman in the first instance (page 84) and as a soldier in the second (page 93). During the First World War, Bruce Bairnsfather included a character he had created by the name of Old

Bill to represent the average Tommy (page 36). Strube included the most famous everyman figure ever created in the form of the 'little man' (page 76) who successfully represented the average man in the street during the 1920s and '30s. Poy, Strube's rival on the *Daily Mail*, also had a man-on-the-Clapham-omnibus-type figure entitled John Citizen who, like the little man, observed and reacted to the political events of the day. Low created two famous allegorical figures, the double-headed ass which represented Lloyd George's coalition government of 1918–22 (page 40), and Colonel Blimp, a symbol of stupidity, mixed-up thinking and diehard reaction (page 87). Low claimed that he developed the character of Blimp after overhearing two rotund military types in a Turkish bath agreeing that cavalry officers should be entitled to wear their spurs inside tanks.

The proverbial phrase about living through 'interesting times' applies directly to great cartoons: the more momentous the event, the higher the standard of the cartoons. Whether in times of war, the threat of terrorism, economic downturn or political uncertainty, our cartoonists have always risen to the unique challenge. What Churchill called Britain's 'finest hour' turned out to be our cartoonists' finest hour too, and that desperate period in 1940 (maybe Britain's darkest moment in history) directly led to many inspirational and memorable cartoons – they assisted in restoring and then maintaining the public's morale, which is the main responsibility of cartoonists during wartime. Our present cohort have, once again, met the unprecedented challenge of adversity, from the coronavirus pandemic, head on. Fortuitously – and unlike most other illnesses – the virus, with its spherical shape surrounded by its crown of club-shaped spikes, has offered them a striking visual image to play with, and has therefore provided unlimited opportunities to chart the response to it by our government and those of other countries around the world.

This anthology is full of truly great political cartoons that continue to inform, educate and amuse. Borrowing David Low's description of himself as 'a nuisance dedicated to sanity', cartoonists today remain a constant force for good by unremittingly holding to account those who try to govern us. Whether cartoons will survive for another three hundred years we cannot predict, but this book surely presents the case that they should.

THE CARTOONS

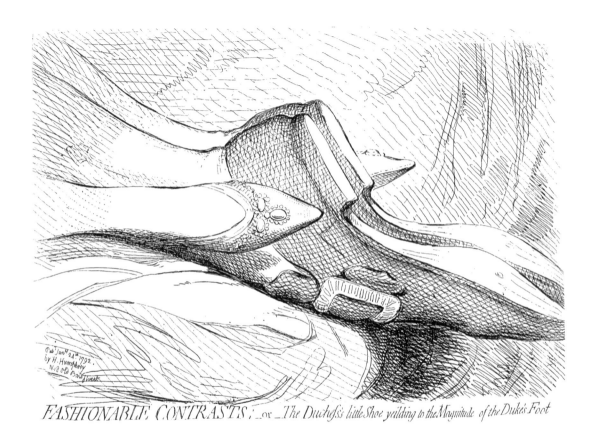

FASHIONABLE CONTRASTS;—or—The Duchess's little Shoe yeilding to the Magnitude of the Duke's Foot

24 January 1792
James Gillray

The British press became fascinated by Frederica Charlotte, the eldest daughter of the King of Prussia, when she married Prince Frederick, George III's second son. Despite lacking aristocratic bearing, the British press, desperate to like her, seized upon another sign of privilege: the extreme daintiness of her footwear. Copies of her tiny shoes were sold as royal souvenirs and, attempting to emulate her, fashionable ladies wore their own shoes ever smaller.

POLITICAL-RAVISHMENT, — or — The Old Lady of Threadneedle-Street in danger!

This print was responsible for giving the Bank of England its nickname: the 'Old Lady of Threadneedle Street'. Prime Minister William Pitt the Younger seduces an elderly woman who represents the Bank of England, in order to get his hands on her gold. Pitt was at the time attempting to reduce the national debt, with his government ordering the Bank of England to issue paper banknotes rather than gold.

22 May 1797
James Gillray

JOHN BULL taking a Luncheon: — or — British Cooks, cramming Old Grumble-Gizzard, with Bonne-Chére.

In this celebration of Nelson's victory at the Battle of the Nile in August 1798, Nelson offers John Bull a dish of conquered French ships. Other dishes representing British naval victories are also proffered. However, John Bull, the 'Old Grumble-Gizzard', is not happy and complains rather ungratefully: 'What! more Frigasees?' The word 'frigasees' is a play on fricassée, a French cooked dish, and frigate, a warship. On the floor, an overflowing jug of True British Stout decorated with the royal arms further reinforces the joy of British superiority, while outside the window members of the Opposition, including Charles James Fox, are seen scampering away.

24 October 1798
James Gillray

4

In arguably Gillray's greatest print, based on Napoleon's unofficial peace offer to George III in January 1805, William Pitt and Napoleon Bonaparte are seen carving up the globe between them. Despite this cynical image of a British prime minister colluding with the French emperor, Napoleon's overtures were rebuffed by the British who made it clear that they would prosecute the war against the French with 'vigour'. This print led to the popular misconception that Napoleon was small in stature despite being of average height. A decade later, while in exile on the island of Elba, Napoleon personally claimed that Gillray's depictions of him 'did more damage than a dozen generals' and that 'he did more than all the armies in Europe to bring me down'.

26 February 1805
James Gillray

Massacre at St Peter's or "BRITONS STRIKE HOME"!!!

In August 1819 a crowd of approximately seventy thousand gathered in St Peter's Field, Manchester, to hear Henry 'Orator' Hunt and other radicals address them on the issue of parliamentary representation. The local magistrates, who had banned the assembly, panicked at the size of the crowd and ordered the military authorities to arrest the speakers; the local yeomanry enthusiastically charged in. An estimated eighteen people, including four women and a child, died from sabre cuts and trampling, while nearly seven hundred were seriously injured. The Peterloo Massacre occurred during a period of immense political tension and mass protests. Fewer than two per cent of the population had the vote, and hunger was rife with the Corn Laws making bread unaffordable for many.

16 August 1819
George Cruikshank

LONDON going out of Town — or — The March of Bricks & mortar!

This print depicts the expansion of London as an invasion of the countryside. Building tools, construction materials and even entire tenement blocks that have magically come to life convey the same anxiety over the speed and scale of early urbanisation.

1 November 1829
George Cruikshank

SUBSTANCE AND SHADOW

Prior to this work by John Leech, cartoons were simply referred to as humorous drawings. The subject here is the upcoming exhibition of fresco designs for the rebuilt Palace of Westminster. Leech felt this exhibition, commissioned by politicians, was a complete waste of public money as London was then a city of poverty, ill health, slums and workhouses, and *Punch* saw it simply as a means for the elite to celebrate their own importance. At the time, a fresco or preliminary sketch was known as a 'cartoon', and Leech's use of the word was intended to ridicule the pretensions of the establishment and their grandiose attitudes. From this point on, *Punch*'s central political illustration was known as the cartoon. The popularity of the *Punch* cartoons led to the term's widespread use, and Leech became known as the first 'cartoonist'.

15 July 1843
John Leech
Punch

CAPITAL AND LABOUR

The first report on child labour, which led to Parliament legislating against the employment underground of all females and of boys under ten years of age, was the inspiration for this cartoon. The report also considered the conditions of children employed in manufacturing, and highlighted the dangerous working practices in factories – for example, children would customarily crawl under textile mill machinery while it was running in order to clear away cotton threads.

12 August 1843
Shallaballa (Robert
Jacob Hamerton)
Punch

9

THE BRITISH LION'S VENGEANCE ON THE BENGAL TIGER

The first representation of women as victims of the Indian mutiny, this cartoon emphasises Britain's need for vengeance on India for the murder and potential rape of women. It received considerable attention at the time, with the *New York Times* describing it in September 1857 as 'emblematic of a near-universal British desire for revenge'. It made the career of John Tenniel, who later achieved fame as the illustrator of *Alice's Adventures in Wonderland*.

22 August 1857
John Tenniel
Punch

'DISHING THE WHIGS'

Benjamin Disraeli used electoral reform as a method of gaining popular support
for the Tory Party. His aim was to 'dish [defeat] the Whigs' by stealing their
Liberal clothes. Disraeli persuaded his supporters that the English working man
would make limited demands on politicians, and if kept housed, fed and clothed
he would vote Conservative for ever. This was an unusual ploy for the Tories
who had been consistently against electoral reform. Disraeli can be seen alongside Lord Derby 'dishing' their Whig opponents by presenting the heads of the
Opposition, including that of Gladstone, on a plate to Queen Victoria.

24 August 1867
Henry E. Doyle
Fun

THE FENIAN GUY FAWKES

In the 1860s Irish–English relations were at a low. Two Fenian (Irish) prisoners were being held at Clerkenwell, situated in a working-class area with a large residential population. Fellow Fenians attempted to blow open the wall of the house of detention in an effort to rescue them. In the explosion, twelve people were killed while 120 others were injured. Tenniel continually depicted rebellious Irishmen – those 'troublesome people' – as ape-like and unkempt malcontents.

28 December 1867
John Tenniel
Punch

12

THAT TROUBLES OUR MONKEY AGAIN

FEMALE DESCENDANT OF MARINE ASCIDIAN: *Really, Mr Darwin, say what you like about man; but I wish you would leave my emotions alone!*

Cartoonists regularly mocked Charles Darwin and his theory of evolution by depicting him as an ape. Distaste at the sexual implications of his theory of shared heredity was played out at length in the popular press, where such images encapsulated Victorian society's sense of unease with the notion that humans had, at some stage, been descended from apes. Darwin himself, however, enjoyed appearing in cartoons.

16 November 1872
John Gordon Thomson
Fun

MOSÉ IN EGITTO!!!

Taking quick advantage of the viceroy of Egypt's bankruptcy, on behalf of the British government Disraeli was able to purchase a controlling interest in the Suez Canal Company. Since Parliament was not in session at the time, he had to borrow the £4 million required from the Rothschild family. Disraeli saw the acquisition of the Suez Canal as vital to serving the interests of both the Indian Empire and British trade. *Mosé in Egitto* (Moses in Egypt) is the title of an opera by Rossini first performed in 1818.

11 December 1875
John Tenniel
Punch

'NEW CROWNS FOR OLD ONES!'

Benjamin Disraeli appears as Abanazer from *Aladdin*, offering Queen Victoria an imperial crown in exchange for her old British one. The prime minister cleverly cultivated a public image of himself as an imperialist, with grand gestures such as conferring on the Queen the title Empress of India.

15 April 1876
John Tenniel
Punch

DROPPING THE PILOT

Otto von Bismarck had tendered his resignation as chancellor of the German Empire to Kaiser Wilhelm II, but had phrased it in such a way as to make clear that he had done so under sufferance. The consequences of his dismissal were disastrous. Wilhelm's rejection of Bismarck's sophisticated approach to foreign policy eventually resulted in war against Britain, France and Russia in August 1914. When Bismarck was given the original of this cartoon, he reportedly commented, 'It is indeed a fine one.'

29 March 1890
John Tenniel
Punch

WILFUL WILHELM

'Take the nasty Punch away!
I won't have any Punch to-day!'

In a fit of pique over depictions of him in *Punch*, Kaiser Wilhelm II cancelled his subscription to the magazine. Wilhelm even wrote to Queen Victoria to express his distaste for cartoons aimed at him and asked his grandmother to halt its publication immediately. The Queen replied that such action was not 'quite within her province', but requested that the editor be made aware of the negative effect the cartoons were having on Anglo-German relations. Linley Sambourne's response was to produce a damning portrait of the kaiser tearing up copies of *Punch*.

26 March 1892
Linley Sambourne
Punch

THE RHODES COLOSSUS

Striding from Cape Town to Cairo

This cartoon became the definitive image of British imperial power. By 1892 Cecil Rhodes's commercial and business interests in South Africa had merged with his message of imperial patriotism as prime minister of the Cape Colony. On 29 November, Rhodes made a speech in which he dramatically announced that he intended to extend the colony's telegraphic connections across the entire continent, not only to Lake Tanganyika and Uganda, but through the fundamentalist Islamic Sudan and all the way to British Cairo.

10 December 1892
Linley Sambourne
Punch

18

THE ASSAULT!!

Despite strong Tory opposition, William Gladstone put his second Irish Home Rule Bill to the House of Commons in 1893. The Tories sided with the Liberal Unionist Party who broke away from the Liberals and Gladstone's support of Home Rule. The bill allowed Irish representatives to enter Parliament but retained Parliament's supremacy on imperial issues. Randolph Churchill and Joseph Chamberlain, among others, are using a battering ram with the head of Lord Salisbury. Gladstone looks on in horror.

18 March 1893
John Tenniel
Punch

19

SHIVERING ON THE BRINK

As colonial secretary, Joseph Chamberlain wanted to strengthen the British Empire by favouring trade with the colonies and imposing tariffs on imports from outside the Empire. Prime Minister Arthur Balfour was reticent as he felt the issue of tariff reform would divide his Tory government. He was right, and in 1906 Sir Henry Campbell-Bannerman's free trade-supporting Liberal Party won a landslide general election victory. Carruthers Gould, the first full-time political cartoonist in Britain, was later knighted by the Liberal government.

5 June 1903
Francis Carruthers Gould
Westminster Gazette

THE COMING PERILETTE

A sky-sign of the times

(A scientist announces the threatened impact of a comet which is to reduce the earth to ashes. Other scientists assert that the earth will easily survive its advent. For the moment the topic has been 'talked out'.)

On 8 March the Women's Enfranchisement Bill was introduced to Parliament for its second reading but was talked out by members of the House of Commons. Twelve days later, seventy-six suffragettes were arrested when the Women's Social and Political Union attempted to storm the Houses of Parliament.

15 March 1907
Bernard Partridge
Punch

21

LEGISLATION BY PYJAMA

There are others besides the landowners of the country who are made to 'sit up' by the budget. (Mr Winston Churchill was supposed to have been discovered on the Treasury Bench in pink pyjamas.)

As president of the Board of Trade, Winston Churchill alongside David Lloyd George and Herbert Asquith took an active role in bringing about the Liberal government's radical social reforms. His direct achievements at the Board of Trade were considerable, particularly in employment law. He was responsible for introducing an eight-hour day in all mines and establishing the first minimum-wage system in Britain. He also set up the first labour exchanges to help unemployed people find work.

25 August 1909
E. T. Reed
Punch

FORCED FELLOWSHIP

SUSPICIOUS-LOOKING PARTY: *Any objection to my company, guv'nor? I'm agoin' your way – (aside) and further.*

Despite having won a landslide victory in 1906, the Liberals were wary of the twenty-nine Labour MPs sitting in the House of Commons whose party had a programme of social reform that was attractive to the working classes. The Liberals felt that if they themselves did not introduce social reform, they might be replaced by the Labour Party at the next election, as an alternative to the Conservatives. The Liberals, committed to the ideal of the minimal state and free market, feared the socialist bureaucracy of a planned economy that Labour would be likely to introduce.

27 October 1909
Bernard Partridge
Punch

THE VANDAL AND HIS BLUDGEON.

(In his letter to Sir George Ritchie the other day, Mr. Churchill said that "the Lords claim that they shall remain possessed of an all-powerful Veto which they can use to harass, damage, and finally dissolve, every Government and every House of Commons of which they are not masters.")

"I'll teach the common herd to prate about their will to me! I, and I alone, am Master here!!"

20 November 1910
Frank Holland
Reynolds' News

When David Lloyd George attempted to introduce a people's budget with higher taxes on unearned income and land taxes disadvantageous to the propertied classes, it was thrown out by the hostile Tory majority in the House of Lords. Lloyd George branded the Lords 'Mr Balfour's poodle'. The stand-off resulted in two general elections, the second of which the Liberals won with a 'peers against the people' campaign slogan.

'FOR WHAT YOU ARE ABOUT TO RECEIVE . . .'

Many imprisoned suffragettes went on hunger strike to protest against the uncompromising Liberal government. The cartoon depicts Home Secretary Reginald McKenna force-feeding a jailed suffragette. McKenna defended the practice as being 'necessary medical treatment' and a deterrent to make suffragettes think twice before carrying out militant actions.

24 May 1913
Will Dyson
Daily Herald

A FANTASY

Labour leaders at their devotions

When Tony Blair became prime minister, he was given the original of this cartoon, a gift from William Mellor, the son of a former editor of the *Daily Herald*. It criticises the contemporary Labour leadership for the unforgivable sin of toadying up to capitalism. Having unwrapped his gift, one of hundreds he received in his first days in office, Blair looked at it and squirmed. He then quickly put it on the 'don't accept' pile saying, 'No, I don't think we want that!'

3 December 1913
Will Dyson
Daily Herald

THE HOLIDAY SEASON AD 1914

Germany declared war on France. The following day, when Britain declared war on Germany, Francis Carruthers Gould produced a prophetic doom-laden cartoon that was to be the only one he ever drew that was refused publication. The editor of the *Westminster Gazette*, John Spender, objected to it as being contrary to public sentiment and, in his words, 'likely to offend'.

4 August 1914
Francis Carruthers Gould
Westminster Gazette
(unpublished)

BRAVO, BELGIUM!

The German attack on Belgium contributed to Britain's decision to enter the war. Much to the kaiser's disappointment, the Belgian army managed to hold off the might of the German army far longer than even the British had anticipated.

12 August 1914
F. H. Townsend
Punch

THE TRIUMPH OF 'CULTURE'

To retaliate for the shelling from the Belgian forts surrounding Liège, German troops rounded up inhabitants from neighbouring villages and shot them; those still alive were finished off with bayonets. By 8 August nearly 850 civilians had been murdered. The British Ministry of Information used these atrocities to instil public hatred of both the kaiser and the German people.

26 August 1914
Bernard Partridge
Punch

A CLEAN SWEEP

MRS BRITANNIA: *It has to be done: so I might just as well do it first as last – and so get rid of all the dangerous microbes.*

In 1914 there were up to fifty thousand German and Austrian nationals residing in Britain. There were fears that they would engage in acts of espionage and sabotage, but the government was initially reluctant to impose internment, choosing instead to restrict the activities of those suspected of being a threat to national security. The term 'concentration camp' was obviously not yet synonymous with the later horrors of the Nazi death camps, although British concentration camps during the Boer War had led to many deaths through starvation and disease.

24 October 1914
J. M. Staniforth
Western Mail

The failure of the Schlieffen Plan led to Germany fighting on two fronts simultaneously. German failure to knock France out of the war quickly led General Moltke to inform the kaiser, 'Sir, we have lost the war.' Haselden had great success depicting Kaiser Wilhelm II and his son Wilhelm in his wartime comic strip, 'The Sad Experiences of Big and Little Willie'. A testament to its popularity was that a prototype of the first British tank was called 'Little Willie'.

10 December 1914
William Haselden
Daily Mirror

GETTING THE SPIKE

On 28 January, off the coast of Brazil, the USS *William P. Frye* was the first American vessel to be sunk by the Germans. A German U-boat torpedoed the British-owned luxury steamship *Lusitania* on 7 May, killing 1,195 people, including 123 Americans. These disasters immediately strained relations between Germany and the neutral United States and would eventually see the US enter the war on the Allied side.

30 January 1915
Poy (Percy Fearon)
Evening News

STUDY OF A PRUSSIAN HOUSEHOLD HAVING ITS MORNING HATE

This cartoon successfully captured the British wartime view of the archetypal humourless, hateful 'Hun' family. It proved so popular it was reproduced as a colour print.

24 February 1915
Frank Reynolds
Punch

ON THE BLACK LIST

KAISER (*as executioner*): *I'm going to hang you.*

PUNCH: *Oh, you are, are you? Well, you don't seem to know how the scene ends. It's the hangman that gets hanged.*

The German daily newspaper *Die Deutsche Tageszeitung* directly issued a warning to *Punch*, probably on the orders of the kaiser who had a long-standing grudge against the magazine. The paper threatened that 'when the day of reckoning arrives we shall know with whom we have to deal and how to deal with them.'

16 June 1915
Leonard Raven-Hill
Punch

VULCAN'S FORGE

VULCAN (*Lloyd George*): *Ah, you wait a bit, my boy! I'm going to fit you up with a set of claws that'll go through anything!*

In May, Lloyd George was made minister of munitions in order to solve the severe arms shortage. It is generally accepted that he boosted national morale as well as the stock of armaments, but it has also been said that the increase in munitions output was largely due to reforms already made before he was appointed.

10 July 1915
E. T. Reed
London Opinion

'WELL, IF YOU KNOWS OF A BETTER 'OLE, GO TO IT.'

Bairnsfather's most famous cartoon was drawn while he was recuperating after being injured in the Second Battle of Ypres. Recalling his time in the trenches, Bairnsfather said he frequently 'saw the satire' in trench-fighters finding themselves 'in such a macabre and pathetic predicament of mutilated landscapes, primitive trench life, ceaseless wearing drudgery' and the 'ever-present danger of the final nuisance'. He commented that his drawings 'emerged as my only means of being articulate about what I felt'.

24 November 1915
Bruce Bairnsfather
Bystander

A WASTED LIFE

KAISER (*to Count Zeppelin*): *Tell me, Count, why didn't you invent something useful, like the 'tanks'?*

Count Ferdinand von Zeppelin had invented the airship which bears his name in 1900, and by 1915 Zeppelins were carrying out raids on targets in eastern England and east and south London. They made little impact, however, because of the inaccuracy of their bombing and the small size of their bombs. By contrast, the tank gave the British the advantage of surprise and terrorised the German defenders, which proved a great propaganda success back home.

27 September 1916
F. H. Townsend
Punch

PEACE AND FUTURE CANNON FODDER

THE TIGER: *Curious! I seem to hear a child weeping!*

This prophetic cartoon not only predicted that the Treaty of Versailles would result in another world war, but also the year (1940) in which hostilities would begin. The leaders of the victorious Allies, David Lloyd George, Vittorio Orlando, Georges Clemenceau (the 'tiger', centre) and Woodrow Wilson, are seen emerging from the Palace of Versailles. As Clement Attlee put it: 'That foreboding was justified.'

17 May 1919
Will Dyson
Daily Herald

THE GAP IN THE BRIDGE

The refusal of the Republican-dominated United States Senate to ratify membership of the League of Nations was a major factor in its demise. President Woodrow Wilson lamented: 'We had a chance to gain the leadership of the world. We have lost it.' Without American participation, the League of Nations was doomed to fail.

10 December 1919
Leonard Raven-Hill
Punch

SOME JUGGLER

David Low created a two-headed ass as a symbol for Lloyd George's Liberal–Conservative coalition government, defining the body more precisely as that of a mule, 'without pride of ancestry or hope of posterity'. In Ireland, Lloyd George attempted to placate both nationalists and unionists with the Government of Ireland Act, which created two governments: one in Belfast with jurisdiction over the six northern counties, and the other in Dublin with authority over the remainder.

19 October 1921
David Low
Star

THE SCAPEGOAT THAT TURNED

MR LLOYD GEORGE AT MANCHESTER: *If I am driven alone into the Wilderness . . .*

MRS LLOYD GEORGE AT EAST HAM: *My husband thoroughly enjoys a fight.*

In the summer of 1922, Lloyd George was involved in a scandal involving the selling of knighthoods and peerages. On 19 October, after his belligerent handling of the threat of war with Turkey, Conservative backbenchers finally voted down the coalition, and Lloyd George resigned after seventeen years in government. Historian A. J. P. Taylor once remarked that Lloyd George was called the 'Welsh wizard' by his admirers and the 'goat' by those who mistrusted him.

25 October 1922
Bernard Partridge
Punch

INTO THE LIMELIGHT

At the 1922 general election, Labour replaced a divided Liberal Party as the main opposition to the Conservatives, with Ramsay MacDonald as party leader. It was the first election where Labour surpassed the combined strength of both sections of the Liberal Party in votes as well as seats.

29 November 1922
Bernard Partridge
Punch

SOCIALISM'S LIBERAL HIGHWAY

After an inconclusive election on 6 December 1923 that the ruling Conservatives lost but nobody won, on 22 January Ramsay MacDonald became both prime minister and foreign secretary of a minority Labour government. Churchill called it 'a national misfortune such as has usually befallen a great state only on the morrow of defeat in war'. The *Daily Mail* begged Liberal leader Herbert Asquith, seen here lying in the path of MacDonald's chariot, to save the country by forming a coalition to keep Labour out. Asquith chose to ignore their call, believing Labour would be shown to be incapable of governing.

16 January 1924
Poy
Daily Mail

ON THE LOAN TRAIL

It is now known that the so-called Zinoviev letter was forged by MI6 and leaked to the *Daily Mail* to damage Labour's chances of winning the general election. The letter, which claimed to be from Grigori Zinoviev, president of the Soviet Comintern, called on British communists to mobilise 'sympathetic forces' in the Labour Party to support an Anglo-Soviet treaty and to encourage 'agitation-propaganda' in the armed forces.

29 October 1924
Bernard Partridge
Punch

THE OLD LOVE AND THE NEW

After winning the 1924 general election, Stanley Baldwin was particularly concerned about Winston Churchill, who he believed would be less of a problem within the Cabinet than outside it causing trouble from the backbenches. Despite Churchill knowing very little about finance, Baldwin named him Chancellor of the Exchequer. The appointment was less popular among the protectionists in the party, who regarded Churchill's recent re-conversion to Conservatism with undisguised suspicion.

16 February 1925
Bernard Partridge
Punch

IS WESTMINSTER CRUMBLING?

The condition of the fabric of the Houses of Parliament is giving cause for much anxiety

The General Strike began after the trade unions came out on strike in sympathy with the miners, who had been locked out by the mine owners because of their refusal to accept a cut in pay and longer working hours. Their demands were immortalised by the words of A. J. Cook, president of the Miners' Federation: 'Not a penny off the pay, not a minute on the day.' Meanwhile, a parliamentary committee found the stonework of the Houses of Parliament to be in dire need of repair.

2 May 1926
Poy
Evening News

THE DARKENING OF THE SUN

British police raided the head-quarters of the Soviet trade delegation in London, searching for top-secret documents that had been stolen from the War Office. This led to diplomatic relations being broken off and raised fears of a war between the two countries. In the Soviet Union, Stalin used this fear to isolate his enemies and push the country towards an accelerated pace of industrialisation.

22 June 1927
Bernard Partridge
Punch

HOIST WITH HIS
OWN ROBOOT

COMRADE TROTSKY: *Why did
I help to make this machine so
efficient?*

In 1925 Stalin had removed
Leon Trotsky from his role as
war commissar, and the following year he dismissed him from
the Politburo. On 12 November,
he expelled him from the
Communist Party. Stalin would
later force Trotsky into exile and
order his assassination.

23 November 1927
Leonard Raven-Hill
Punch

DARWIN KNEW!

A bill was introduced to give all women the vote on the same terms as men, which if passed would have meant that women would constitute almost fifty-three per cent of the British electorate. The *Daily Mail* complained that these impressionable young females would be easily manipulated by the Labour Party. There was little opposition to the bill in Parliament and the Equal Franchise Act became law on 2 July 1928. As a result, all women over the age of twenty-one could now vote in elections.

30 March 1928
Poy
Daily Mail

AND A PULL ALL TOGETHER

A financial crisis had led to a split within the Labour government, with nine ministers resigning rather than accepting cuts to unemployment benefits. George V asked Ramsay MacDonald to stay on as prime minister and form a national government, which he did on 24 August. Party leaders, as seen here, Herbert Samuel (Liberal) and Stanley Baldwin (Tory), joined MacDonald in a Conservative-dominated coalition which divided the Labour Party; John Bull is the anchorman in the cartoon.

SEARCHING THE VAULTS: THIS YEAR WE IMAGINE IT WILL TAKE A MAGNIFYING GLASS TO FIND ANYTHING!

The 1931 general election, which took place on 27 October, made a mockery of the adversarial system, returning a 550-strong coalition government led by MacDonald but almost entirely dominated by Conservatives. Labour, in their worst ever electoral performance, saw their Commons representation plummet from 289 seats to just 52. Seventy-three-year-old George Lansbury, the only former Labour Cabinet minister to save his seat, assumed the leadership of the Labour Party. He was universally known as a committed socialist and pacifist.

10 November 1931
Poy
Evening News

51

OSWALD FOR ENGLAND

SIR OSWALD MOSLEY:
Gentleman and fellow-patriots,
you see what the other Duce is
going to do for Europe? Well, I
myself engage to do the same for
England. You may put your black
shirts on that.

After a visit to Italian dictator
Benito Mussolini, Sir Oswald
Mosley founded the British
Union of Fascists in October.
Mosley concluded that only fas-
cism provided the wherewithal
to 'save' Britain from ruin and
a possible communist takeover.
The BUF quickly developed the
appearance of a major political
party, with a membership of
forty thousand, but its progress
was hindered by violent public
confrontation between the BUF
and its opponents.

"WITHIN TEN YEARS
EUROPE WILL BE
EITHER FASCISTS
OR FASCITIZED."
MUSSOLINI
AT MILAN

2 November 1932
Leonard Raven-Hill
Punch

THE DOORMAT.

In 1931, a supposed Chinese act of aggression in Manchuria, dubbed the Mukden Incident, led Japan to respond with a full invasion of the Chinese territory. By doing so, Japan had broken the oath of non-aggression that it had sworn to the League of Nations. Japan's failure to comply with any proposed resolutions by the League should have resulted in economic sanctions and collective military enforcement by its members. The League failed to act, however.

19 January 1933
David Low
Evening Standard

THE TEMPORARY TRIANGLE

On 30 January President Hindenburg finally made Adolf Hitler chancellor of Germany after initially refusing to do so. In a series of negotiations, former Chancellor Franz von Papen convinced Hindenburg to appoint Hitler, with the understanding that non-Nazis in government would contain him. From that moment, there was little Hindenburg, von Papen or, indeed, anyone could do to stop the creation of a Nazi dictatorship.

8 February 1933
Bernard Partridge
Punch

On 27 February, the German Reichstag building burned down due to arson. Hitler and the Nazis exploited the fire to persuade President Hindenburg that Communists were planning a violent uprising. They claimed that emergency legislation was needed to prevent this. Commonly known as the Reichstag Fire Decree, the resulting act paved the way for the Nazi dictatorship of Germany.

1 March 1933
Poy
Evening News

HIS MORNING EXERCISE

The lone ex-minister upon his elephant

Winston Churchill founded the India Defence League in order to oppose giving greater independence to India. His reactionary views on India alienated him from all three main political parties, with many now believing his political career was all but over. This resulted in his later warnings about the dangers of Nazism going largely unheeded.

8 March 1933
Leonard Raven-Hill
Punch

ALL FOOLS' DAY IN GERMANY

CHANCELLOR HITLER: *As a retaliation for the false statement by foreigners that we have been persecuting the Jews, I forbid you to enter the shop.*

Less than three months after coming to power in Germany, Adolf Hitler permitted an organised boycott of Jewish businesses while also beginning to exclude Jews from public life. The boycott was presented to the German people as an act of revenge for German and foreign Jews accused of spreading atrocity stories to damage Germany's reputation.

5 April 1933
Bernard Partridge
Punch

KONG!

(With acknowledgements to the film)

Set up by the League of Nations, the Disarmament Conference finally opened in Geneva. Although sixty countries attended the conference, it was severely weakened by the absence of the United States and Russia. Hitler's demand that German armaments be allowed to reach parity with those of France was refused and, as a consequence, he withdrew Germany from the conference and from the League of Nations, while beginning a programme of rapid rearmament. Meanwhile, *King Kong* had just opened in British cinemas.

10 May 1933
Sidney Strube
Daily Express

THEY SALUTE WITH BOTH HANDS NOW.

This cartoon reflects the aftermath of 30 June when, on Hitler's orders, Himmler's SS and Göring's special police purged the Nazi party by arresting and executing the leaders of the Brown Shirts, or SA, under its head, Ernst Röhm. Röhm was one of many to perish in the 'Night of the Long Knives'.

3 July 1934
David Low
Evening Standard

YOICKS!

The election campaign starts today

Beset by ill health, Ramsay MacDonald stepped down as prime minister on 7 June and was replaced by Conservative Stanley Baldwin, who called a general election within months. The result was a reduced majority for the national government coalition, with the Conservatives remaining the largest party with 387 seats. The National Liberal's vote held up with the loss of just two seats, but National Labour lost five of their thirteen, including that of their leader, Ramsay MacDonald.

26 October 1935
Poy
Daily Mail

" YOU KNOW YOU CAN TRUST ME "

Prime Minister Stanley Baldwin spoke publicly of the importance of the League of Nations and supported sanctions against Italy after the conquest of Abyssinia. However, Foreign Secretary Sir Samuel Hoare entered into a secret agreement with French Premier Pierre Laval to recognise fully Mussolini's annexation of Abyssinia. Details of the pact leaked and were widely denounced as appeasement of Italian aggression. In a radio broadcast Baldwin had appealed to the public to trust him: 'I am a man of peace. I am longing, and looking and praying for peace . . . Cannot you trust me to ensure a square deal and to ensure even justice between man and man?'

20 December 1935
David Low
Evening Standard

THE GOOSE-STEP

'Goosey goosey gander
Whither dost thou wander?'
'Only through the Rhineland—
Pray excuse my blunder!'

On 7 March Hitler ordered the reoccupation of the Rhineland in contravention of the Treaty of Locarno. Even though he only sent a token military force there, Britain and France did nothing to stop him, so demonstrating their timidity and the weakness of the League of Nations. The nursery rhyme 'Goosey Goosey Gander' is used here to emphasise the goose-step, a marching step heavily associated with the German army at the time.

18 March 1936
E. H. Shepard
Punch

STEPPING STONES TO GLORY.

Britain and France's continuing appeasement of Germany led Hitler to become further emboldened in his attempt to achieve his foreign policy aims in Europe. The cartoonist predicted that without resistance Hitler would continue to take steps to strengthen his position, and this was indeed proven to be the case as he went on to swallow up Austria, Czechoslovakia and Poland before the European democracies finally stood up to him.

8 July 1936
David Low
Evening Standard

THE SPANISH SEE-SAW

MR EDEN: *This may be a new 'balance of power', but it certainly isn't 'collective security'.*

In July civil war had broken out in Spain. Stanley Baldwin and French Premier Leon Blum called for European states to abstain from intervening, and twenty-seven countries, including Germany, Italy and the USSR, signed a non-intervention agreement, although all three subsequently broke it. Foreign Secretary Anthony Eden remained undecided as to which side should be supported.

2 December 1936
Bernard Partridge
Punch

HESITATION

After reigning for less than a year, Edward VIII became the first English monarch to abdicate voluntarily. He decided to do so after the government and the Church of England condemned his decision to marry the American divorcée Wallis Simpson. Choosing her over the throne, he said: 'I have found it impossible to carry the heavy burden of responsibility and to discharge my duties as king, as I would wish to do, without the help and support of the woman I love.' The next day his younger brother, the Duke of York, became King George VI.

9 December 1936
E. H. Shepard
Punch

WILL HE MAKE A CLEAN SWEEP?

Opinion in government circles favours a general election to test the feeling of the country on the premier's Munich policy

Neville Chamberlain returned from Munich claiming to have averted war with Germany and brought back 'peace for our time'. The Scottish socialist MP James Maxton said that he had done 'something that the mass of the common people of the world wanted done'. Chamberlain was feted by crowds and floral tributes were sent to Downing Street. Despite the public's euphoria that Britain had avoided war, there was a feeling of growing unease as the Nazis went on to dismember Czechoslovakia.

5 October 1938
J. C. Walker
South Wales Echo

___ ___ AND THE SEVEN DWARFS

Chamberlain's accommodating stance over Czechoslovakia convinced Hitler that the British would not seriously resist further annexations in the east, and he turned his attention to the former Prussian city of Danzig, which was surrounded by Polish territory. Hitler intended to use Danzig as a catalyst to provoke war with Poland, stating: 'I shall crush the Poles without warning in such a way that no trace of Poland can be found afterwards. I shall strike with the full force of a mechanised army, of which the Poles have no conception.'

21 December 1938
Bernard Partridge
Punch

'BUT YOU TOLD ME IT WAS STUFFED!'

On 1 September German troops invaded Poland. Having planned for a limited conflict, Hitler did not expect Britain to intervene and was therefore dumbfounded when he learned of the ultimatum of 3 September. It is believed he turned to his Foreign Minister, Joachim von Ribbentrop, and asked, 'What now?', implying that Ribbentrop had misled him about Britain's possible reaction. Ribbentrop's only response was that they were also likely to receive an ultimatum from the French.

4 September 1939
Sidney Strube
Daily Express

RENDEZVOUS

The Nazi-Soviet Pact of August 1939 stunned the world. Two ideological regimes that had for years seen the other as the true enemy had come together to sign a non-aggression pact. The words uttered by Hitler and Stalin are based on those supposedly used by Henry Morton Stanley at his meeting with David Livingstone in 1871.

20 September 1939
David Low
Evening Standard

THE BUS

On 5 April Prime Minister Neville Chamberlain had felt sufficiently confident to declare to the House of Commons that Hitler had 'missed the bus'. However, he was made to eat his words after the Allied military failure in Norway. There was now heightened dissatisfaction and criticism of Chamberlain's conduct of the war. When he entered the House of Commons on the day this cartoon appeared, many Labour MPs greeted him with shouts of 'Missed the bus! Missed the bus!'

7 May 1940
Leslie Illingworth
Daily Mail

'ANY MORE FOR THE SKYLARK?'

Being a tribute to the fishermen who helped to rescue the BEF from Dunkirk

To rescue the French and British troops trapped by the German army in the French port of Dunkirk, all sorts of small vessels, including fishing boats, sailing dinghies and pleasure steamers, crossed the Channel to take troops off the beaches. Over 800 boats helped ferry a total of 338,226 soldiers to Royal Navy ships waiting in deeper waters.

8 June 1940
Spot (Arthur Potts)
Bristol Evening World

Churchill had replaced
Chamberlain as prime minister
on 10 May. After the evacu-
ation of the BEF from Dunkirk,
Britain stood alone against the
might of Nazi Germany. On 4
June, with a German invasion
of Britain believed imminent,
Churchill made his defiant
speech: 'We shall fight on
the beaches, we shall fight on
the landing grounds, we shall
fight in the fields and in the
streets, we shall fight in the
hills . . .' The slogan 'Go to it'
was often used by the Ministry
of Information on propaganda
posters.

8 June 1940
Sidney Strube
Daily Express

"VERY WELL , ALONE "

Despite the fall of France to the Nazi invaders and the 'deliverance' at Dunkirk, Churchill was determined that Britain would fight on alone. Lord Beaverbrook gave the original of this cartoon to Sir John Slessor, who was at the time air chief marshal responsible for Coastal Command, but before doing so Beaverbrook asked Churchill to sign it.

18 June 1940
David Low
Evening Standard

'ALUMINIUMING 'IM'

Your aluminium will help to foil the invasion – turn it in now!

Minister of Aircraft Production Lord Beaverbrook was concerned over the shortage of materials for the construction of fighter aircraft, and came up with the idea of asking the general public to donate all their old aluminium pots and pans. This would also make civilians feel that they were 'doing their bit' and help lift public morale.

11 July 1940
Spot
Bristol Evening World

THE ROMAN STEP

When Mussolini declared war on Britain on 10 June, his forces in East Africa vastly outnumbered those of the British. Despite this, the Italians were slow to get going. In July they pushed tentatively into Sudan, but then stopped when confronted by a British garrison of only four Indian and African battalions, with the 2nd Battalion, the Black Watch, on its way.

14 July 1940
Lees (Peter Walmesley)
Sunday Graphic

'Is it all right now, Henry?'
'Yes, not even scratched.'

Over two million Anderson
shelters, named after Home
Secretary Sir John Anderson,
were erected and, in true
British fashion, made homely
with bunks inside and flowers
and vegetables planted in
the protective banks of earth.
However, only those with
gardens in which to erect them,
less than twenty-five per cent of
the population, benefited from
their provision. An American
journalist wrote during the Blitz
that 'there was a greater danger of
being hit by a vegetable marrow
falling off the roof of an air-raid
shelter than of being struck by
a bomb'.

29 August 1940
Sidney Strube
Daily Express

THE ROCK AND THE STORM

The Germans knew that to invade Britain successfully they would need to eliminate the RAF and thus gain control of the skies above the English Channel. The head of the Luftwaffe, Reich Marshal Hermann Göring, assured Hitler, 'The RAF will be destroyed in time for Operation Sea Lion to be launched by September 15', and he ordered a series of attacks now known as the Battle of Britain. The Luftwaffe estimated haughtily that it would be able to defeat Fighter Command in southern England in four days and destroy the rest of the RAF in four weeks.

25 September 1940
E. H. Shepard
Punch

'WHAT, ME? NO, I NEVER <u>TOUCH</u> GOLDFISH.'

17 November 1940
Leslie Illingworth
Daily Mail

With Poland occupied by Germany and the Soviet Union, Hitler and Stalin turned their attention towards the Balkan states. Romania and Greece, however, had been given unilateral guarantees of military support by the British and French shortly after the dismemberment of Czechoslovakia.

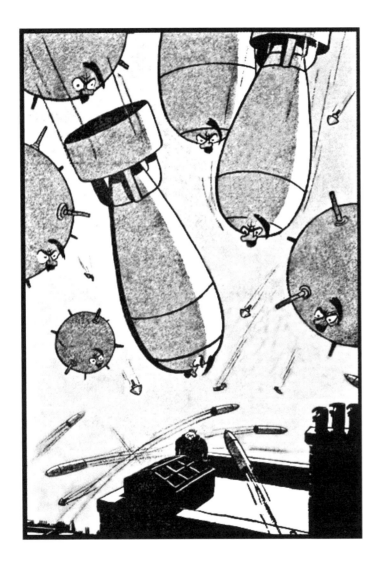

ROOF SPOTTING: THE 2 A.M. FEELING

The Luftwaffe dropped 100,000 incendiary bombs on London in one night, causing unprecedented damage to the city. The area devastated by the ensuing firestorm after just three and a half hours of bombing was larger than that destroyed in the Great Fire of London in 1666, and became known as the 'Second Great Fire of London'. During the Blitz, Giles often worked with bombs falling around him – one went through the top floor of the Reynolds' News building when he was inside, but luckily did not explode.

29 December 1940
Carl Giles
Reynolds' News

Despite Hitler's non-aggression pact with Stalin, Germany invaded the Soviet Union (Operation Barbarossa) on 22 June. Until this point the British had been uncertain whether or not to deal with the Soviet Union whose pact with the Nazis had allowed Hitler to wage war in the first place, but Winston Churchill had no such qualms: 'If Hitler invaded Hell, then I would at least make a favourable reference to the Devil in the House of Commons.' This set the tone of official British reaction, and an Anglo-Soviet agreement was made whereby the two countries now became allies.

23 June 1941
Leslie Illingworth
Daily Mail

'AND WHEN YOU COME TO THINK THAT HITLER RECKONS THE GERMANS ARE THE SUPERIOR HUMAN RACE—'

Holland was occupied by the German army from May 1940. However, after the invasion of Russia in June, the best of the troops were sent to the Eastern Front. Hitler had long believed that Germans were superior to all other races, and in his mind the 'Aryan' race had a duty to control the world. The ideal Aryan had pale skin, blond hair and blue eyes. Non-Aryans were seen as impure and thus inferior. Ironically Hitler thought very highly of the Dutch people, who were considered to be fellow members of the Aryan master race.

9 November 1941
Carl Giles
Reynolds' News

DEATH TAKES A HOLIDAY

The Japanese launched a surprise attack on the United States naval base at Pearl Harbor. This directly led to President Roosevelt declaring war on the Japanese, stating that 7 December 1941 was a date that would live in 'infamy'. On 11 December Hitler declared war on the United States, despite being under no obligation to do so under the mutual defence terms of the Tripartite Pact.

9 December 1941
Leslie Illingworth
Daily Mail

THE SPOILS OF VICTORY

'Your Christmas tree, Führer – I have walked all the way from Russia to bring it to you.'

The German army's first defeat came in the Battle of Moscow. Germany's high command had seriously underestimated the Russians, assuming that German forces would defeat the Soviet army as quickly as they had defeated the French a year earlier. They believed it would be a matter of weeks before they got to Moscow but, instead, they faced substantial and increasing resistance as the Russian counter-attack inflicted heavy casualties.

24 December 1941
Bernard Partridge
Punch

THE PRICE OF PETROL HAS BEEN INCREASED BY ONE PENNY – OFFICIAL

Prime Minister Winston Churchill was furious when the *Daily Mirror* published this cartoon on the government's decision to increase the price of petrol, believing it suggested that merchant seamen's lives had been put at stake to enhance the profits of the petrol companies. In the House of Commons Herbert Morrison, the home secretary, called it a 'wicked cartoon' and 'worthy of Goebbels at his best'. The government considered closing down the *Daily Mirror* but eventually decided to let the newspaper off with a severe reprimand.

6 March 1942
Philip Zec
Daily Mirror

'OK BOYS, WE'LL SHOOT THAT SCENE ONCE MORE – AND THIS TIME LET'S HAVE SOME REAL ACTION.'

Pinewood Studios was selected as the headquarters of the Army Film and Photographic Unit to produce propaganda films for the Ministry of Information. It was here that soldiers were trained in recording events at the Front. From these studios cameramen travelled with various regiments to record the British Army in action. In early 1942, thirty men were sent to Cairo to record the British offensive against the German Africa Korps following the First Battle of El Alamein.

26 July 1942
Carl Giles
Reynolds' News

GOOD AND BAD GERMANS

16 August 1942
Sid Moon
Sunday Dispatch

Intended to strengthen the British resolve against Germany, the Ministry of Information launched an 'Anger Campaign' to instil 'personal anger . . . against the German people and Germany', because the British were 'harbouring little sense of real personal animus against the average German'. Sir Robert Vansittart, the Foreign Office's chief diplomatic adviser, gave a series of radio broadcasts in which he said that Germany was a nation raised on 'envy, self-pity and cruelty', whose historical development had 'prepared the ground for Nazism' and that it was Nazism that had 'finally given expression to the blackness of the German soul'. A popular slogan of the time was: 'The only good German is a dead German.'

Learie Constantine, a member of the West Indian cricket team (who had lived mainly in Lancashire since 1929), was refused entry to a hotel in London's Bloomsbury because white American troops were staying there at the time; American troops were segregated throughout the Second World War. Constantine successfully sued the hotel company in a case which commentators recognise as a milestone in British racial equality. Among later distinctions, Constantine became the first black life peer. This is one of the earliest cartoons to attack colour discrimination.

7 September 1943
David Low
Evening Standard

'THEY SAY, CAN WE DO TWO HUNDRED AND EIGHTY-SEVEN DAINTY AFTERNOON TEAS?'

2 February 1944
Rowland Emett
Punch

In preparation for D-Day, by the spring of 1944 southern England resembled a vast military camp that housed more than one and a half million US servicemen. Much of what was needed to outfit, feed and arm that number of soldiers, sailors and airmen was shipped across the Atlantic.

'FIELD MARSHAL ROMMEL, I PRESUME.'

On 6 June the D-Day landings took place on the Normandy coast of France. General Bernard Montgomery, in command of British and Canadian units, was given the task of taking on the main bulk of the German forces in Normandy commanded by Field Marshal Erwin Rommel. After the success of the Allied landings, he held Rommel's forces at bay while the Americans moved deeper into France to head off the breakout from Normandy. A week after D-Day, this cartoon was requested by – and subsequently given to – Montgomery.

10 June 1944
Sidney Strube
Daily Express

'ELEVEN'-LEAGUE BOOTS

Churchill travelled all over the world building and sustaining the 'Grand Alliance'. He went to Moscow to discuss with Stalin the balance of power and influence both of their countries should have in the Balkans after the war, and then flew to Quebec to meet Roosevelt for their eighth summit of the war. In European folklore, a person wearing seven-league boots could take strides of seven leagues per step, resulting in great speed.

18 October 1944
Bernard Partridge
Punch

"TO BE CANDID I'D BE QUITE SATISFIED IF THEY RESTORED OUR PROPERTY AT THE PRE-WAR VALUATION."

SPECULATION

At the Yalta Conference Churchill, Roosevelt and Stalin held discussions on how the soon-to-be-defeated Axis powers, Germany and Italy, should be governed at the end of the war. The outcome of the conference had wide-ranging implications for the twentieth-century world, from the Korean War to Britain's relationship with the European Union, and resulted in the foundation of the United Nations.

11 February 1945
J. C. Walker
News of the World

In his infamous broadcast of 4 June, Winston Churchill claimed a Labour government would have to employ a form of Gestapo to implement its policies; this was a major miscalculation of public opinion. Labour leader Clement Attlee, a moderate and unassuming man, had been responsible for much of Britain's domestic policy during the war and knew exactly what most people now wanted to be the focus of the new government. Labour ministers such as Minister of Labour Ernest Bevin and Home Secretary Herbert Morrison had also proved themselves capable. Attlee sarcastically thanked Churchill for showing the electorate the difference between the war leader and the party leader.

6 June 1945
Vicky (Victor Weisz)
News Chronicle

Daily Mirror

FORWARD WITH THE PEOPLE

No. 12,900   ONE PENNY
Registered at G.P.O. as a Newspaper.

THUR
JULY 5
1945

DON'T LOSE IT AGAIN

Vote for them

WE reproduce on this page Zec's famous VE-Day cartoon. We do so because it expresses more poignantly than words could do the issues which face the people of this country today.

As you, the electors, with whom the destiny of the nation rests, go to the poll, there will be a gap in your ranks. The men who fought and died that their homeland and yours might live will not be there. You must vote for THEM. Others, happily spared, are unable for various reasons to have their rightful say in this election. You must represent them.

Vote on behalf of the men who won the victory for you. You failed to do so in 1918. The result is known to all. The land "fit for heroes" did not come into existence. The dole did. Short-lived prosperity gave way to long, tragic years of poverty and unemployment. Make sure that history does not repeat itself. Your vote gives you the power. Use it. Let no one turn your gaze to the past. March forward to new and happier times. The call of the men who have gone comes to you. Pay heed to it. Vote for THEM.

Remember the issues. They are national not personal. Your own interest, the future of your children, the welfare of the whole country demand that today you do your duty and

VOTE

"*Here you are—don't lose it again!*"

(Reproduced from our VE-Day Issue without apology.)

This cartoon first appeared on 8 May, the day the war against Germany ended. It was used again, as seen here, on the front page of the *Daily Mirror* on the morning of the 1945 general election, with the text suggesting that the best way to preserve peace was to vote for the Labour Party. Zec's VE Day cartoon summed up the mood of the general public. The *Daily Mirror* was inspired by a letter from a reader, Mrs C. Gardiner, who wrote about the hopes she had when her soldier husband returned home, ending with the pledge 'I shall vote for him.' The paper took up the theme on its front page, with the words 'Vote for them'. The paper's editor, Hugh Cudlipp, said that the cartoon was more influential than any other factor in helping Labour win the 1945 election.

5 July 1945
Philip Zec
Daily Mirror

TWO CHURCHILLS

The British people rejected Winston Churchill as a peacetime prime minister but applauded him as the man who had won the war. This memorable cartoon sums up Churchill's success as a war leader in contrast to his record as a politician. His wife Clementine tried to ease the blow of her husband's election defeat by commenting that it might have been a blessing in disguise, to which he had quickly retorted: 'At the moment it seems quite effectively disguised.'

31 July 1945
David Low
Evening Standard

PEEP UNDER THE IRON CURTAIN

On 5 March Churchill was invited to accept an honorary degree in Fulton, Missouri. In a famous speech he warned that 'an iron curtain' had been placed across Europe and that every Eastern European country behind this iron curtain had fallen, or would soon fall, under the Soviet Union's influence. Stalin made a personal response, in which he accused the former prime minister of being 'a firebrand of war'. Churchill's speech marked, for many, the beginning of the Cold War.

6 March 1946
Leslie Illingworth
Daily Mail

VERDICT AT NUREMBERG

2 October 1946
Gabriel (Jimmy Friell)
Daily Worker

The day before this cartoon was published, twelve leading Nazis were sentenced to death at Nuremberg, including Martin Bormann who was tried *in absentia*. Those to be hung were Göring, von Ribbentrop, Keitel, Rosenberg, Kaltenbrunner, Frank, Frick, Streicher, Sauckel, Seyss-Inquart and Jodl. Göring cheated the hangman by taking cyanide hours before his execution.

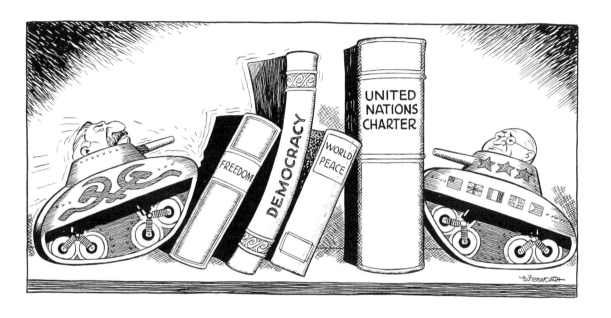

STRAIGHTENING THE BOOKS

On 25 June the North Koreans, with the tacit approval of the Soviet Union, unleashed a surprise attack on South Korea. The United Nations was quick to respond and immediately encouraged its members to come to South Korea's defence. Two days later, without asking Congress to declare war, President Harry Truman ordered United States forces to stop the invading North Korean army as part of the UN police action.

29 June 1950
George Butterworth
Daily Dispatch

MORNING AFTER

3 June 1953
David Low
Guardian

Low's criticism of the extravagance and cost of the coronation of Queen Elizabeth II led to him receiving sack loads of hate mail. The following day, A. P. Wadsworth, editor of the *Guardian*, felt the need to formally apologise in the paper for the cartoon.

'ONE MAN IN HIS TIME PLAYS MANY PARTS.'

The quotation for the caption is from Jacques's speech in Shakespeare's *As You Like It*, beginning 'All the world's a stage', an apt description for Winston Churchill's momentous and long life. Queen Elizabeth II had just honoured him with a knighthood. In the same year he won the Nobel Prize in Literature for his historical and biographical works and for his oratory. More than two thousand readers of the *Sunday Times* applied for reproductions of this cartoon. The newspaper also used it as a cover for the birthday card it sent to Churchill.

29 November 1953
Sidney Strube
Sunday Times

MAN GOETH FORTH UNTO HIS WORK AND TO HIS LABOUR UNTIL THE EVENING

The cartoon shows a seventy-nine-year-old Winston Churchill listless at his desk, his face registering unmistakable effects of a partial paralysis he had suffered the preceding summer, the book-case of his writings full and closed. Churchill was bitterly hurt by the cartoon: 'Yes, there's malice in it. Look at my hands – I have beauti-ful hands . . . *Punch* goes every-where. I shall have to retire if this sort of thing goes on.' Churchill's doctor, Lord Moran, was also shocked by what he considered a vicious caricature of the prime minister: 'There was something un-English in this savage attack on his failing powers. The eyes were dull and lifeless. There was no tone in the flaccid muscles; the jowl sagged. It was the expression-less mask of extreme old age.'

3 February 1954
Leslie Illingworth
Punch

100

DITCHED!

In July, after the United States and Britain had turned down President Nasser of Egypt's request for a loan to fund the building of the Aswan Dam, he nationalised the Suez Canal, saying that he would use the revenue raised to help finance the dam. Determined to regain control of the canal, Britain and France hatched a secret plan with Israel, whereby Israel would invade Egypt and an Anglo-French force would then intervene to 'restore' peace.

2 August 1956
Neville Colvin
Daily Sketch

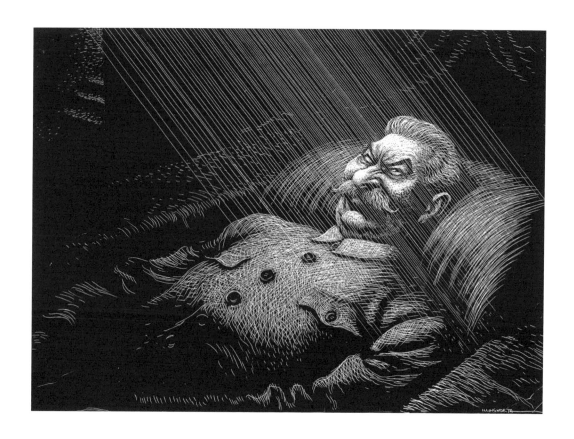

VICTOR OF BUDAPEST

2 November 1956
Leslie Illingworth
Daily Mail

On 23 October, the Hungarian people attempted to overthrow the pro-Soviet regime in Budapest. Nikita Khrushchev took advantage of international disunity over the Suez Crisis by sending 6,000 Russian tanks to Hungary in order to crush the uprising. As a consequence 30,000 Hungarians lost their lives. Doubts were cast thereby on the progress of Khrushchev's de-Stalinisation crusade.

FIRST CASUALTIES

Anthony Eden had vowed to reclaim the 'great imperial lifeline', and Britain and France secretly colluded with Israel in order to take control of the Suez Canal zone. After Israel attacked Egypt in the Sinai as agreed, Britain and France invaded, 'supposedly' to separate the Egyptian forces from the Israelis. When the United States made it clear that it was against any form of military action to resolve the Suez Crisis and put economic pressure on Britain, the humiliated Eden withdrew British forces.

4 November 1956
Neville Colvin
Daily Sketch

After the Suez debacle Anthony Eden resigned and was replaced by Harold Macmillan. To many, Macmillan's demeanour as an Edwardian aristocrat seemed completely out of step with the times. Vicky ridiculed the then prime minister as 'Supermac', a spoof on the American comic strip hero, Superman. Contrary to the cartoonist's intention, the title Supermac ironically benefited Macmillan as he went on to increase his parliamentary majority at the 1959 general election.

6 November 1958
Vicky
Evening Standard

The decolonisation of Africa took place in the late 1950s, with sudden and radical regime changes on the continent as colonial governments made the transition to independent states. Harold Macmillan's later 'wind of change' speech accepted that the days of the British Empire were over, and it dramatically speeded up the process of African independence.

11 March 1959
Ronald Searle
Punch

29 October 1962
Vicky
Evening Standard

During the Cuban Missile Crisis, the United States and the Soviet Union engaged in a tense nuclear stand-off over the installation of nuclear-armed Soviet missiles on Cuba, only ninety miles from the American mainland. Britain, with Harold Macmillan as prime minister, found itself powerless to affect the course of events.

'WHERE NOW?'

On 14 January General de Gaulle (described by the Foreign Office as an 'almost impossible ally') ruthlessly vetoed Britain's bid to join the Common Market. It was a blow that delayed Britain's entry for a decade and hastened the end of Harold Macmillan's political career.

16 January 1963
Leslie Illingworth
Daily Mail

107

7 June 1963
Michael Cummings
Daily Express

John Profumo's affair with a Soho showgirl forced him to resign as Secretary of State for War amid a scandal involving sex, Cold War espionage and suicide. Profumo lied about the affair to Parliament, stating that there was 'no impropriety whatsoever' in his relationship with Christine Keeler. Macmillan continued in office but the scandal was pivotal in his eventual downfall. The editor of the *Daily Express* was unhappy with the first draft of this cartoon, in which Cummings had drawn Keeler as a mermaid with bare bosoms, and told him to cover her vital parts as it was a 'respectable family paper'. Cummings did so with the addition of 'masses of tumbling hair'.

'THERE, I THINK THAT'LL HOLD HIM.'

On 12 June the leader of the anti-apartheid struggle in South Africa, Nelson Mandela, was jailed for life for sabotage. This cartoon shows the Lilliputian figure of Prime Minister Hendrik Verwoerd (later assassinated) watching the placing of restraint on the latent power of black nationalism.

15 June 1964
Leslie Illingworth
Daily Mail

109

'PUT IT THERE, PAL!'

At a meeting at the White House, President Lyndon Johnson asked Britain's new Prime Minister Harold Wilson for military support in Vietnam. Wilson refused as Britain's armed forces were already overstretched, and with a tiny majority in the House of Commons he knew such a proposition would split the Labour Party. Wilson did, however, need American assistance in propping up the pound and Johnson considered tying in financial support for British presence on the ground in Vietnam. Johnson grew frustrated with Wilson over the lack of British cooperation.

6 December 1964
John Jensen
Sunday Telegraph

Labour's attempt to portray the Conservatives as 'yesterday's men' during the 1970 general election campaign backfired badly on them, as this cartoon shows. The following year *Yesterday's Men* was to be the title of a BBC programme about Harold Wilson and his Shadow Cabinet – much to Wilson's fury.

20 June 1970
Les Gibbard
Guardian

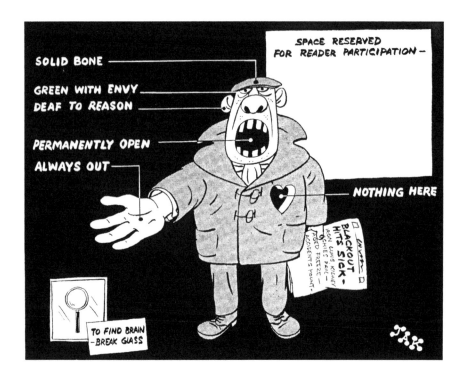

HOMO-ELECTRICAL-SAPIENS BRITANNICUS, CIRCA 1970

Britain suffered its worst power cuts for years, brought about by electricity workers. In December, hospitals were forced to function on batteries and candles during a work-to-rule strike. This cartoon attacking the unions brought an immediate protest from the *Evening Standard*'s printers, who stopped the presses. Production was resumed only when the paper agreed to carry a letter next to Jackson's cartoon, giving the printers' opinion that it was 'beyond the bounds of humour and fair comment'.

9 December 1970
Jak (Raymond Jackson)
Evening Standard

'I'M NOT SURE THAT "WHO GOVERNS BRITAIN?" IS A QUESTION WE SHOULD DRAW ATTENTION TO!'

The failure of Edward Heath's Conservative government to resolve the industrial disputes that blighted Britain's economy forced him to go to the country, seeking a fresh mandate which would enable him to take the unions to task. He called an election with the question, 'Who governs Britain – the unions or the government?' The answer was a hung Parliament; Harold Wilson returned to power with a minority Labour government.

18 January 1974
Nicholas Garland
New Statesman

4 November 1974
Trog (Wally Fawkes)
Observer

The White House released transcripts of subpoenaed tape recordings which disclosed that in June 1972 President Richard Nixon and his chief of staff, H. R. Haldeman, had discussed a plan to use the CIA to thwart the FBI's Watergate investigation. The revelation of the tapes led to Nixon's resignation.

'DON'T WORRY, FOLKS, WE'RE IN CHARGE!'

Labour dubiously won a motion on nationalising the shipbuilding and aircraft
industries by just one vote: 304 to 303. This was because one Labour MP failed
to abstain, in contravention of a pairing arrangement. When Labour MPs
started singing 'The Red Flag', Michael Heseltine, known as Tarzan because of
his mane of golden hair and self-assurance, did the unthinkable. He seized the
ornate mace and brandished it defiantly at the Labour benches.

30 May 1976
Leslie Illingworth
News of the World

'TO TALK ABOUT THE LIBERAL LIFEBLOOD DRAINING AWAY IS NONSENSE' – DAVID STEEL

The Lib–Lab pact came under increasing tension because Labour MPs opposed the call by many Liberals for proportional representation. As a result, Steel soon announced that the pact would end at the close of the parliamentary session. Franklin depicted Labour Prime Minister James Callaghan as the ever-hopeful Micawber from *David Copperfield*. Callaghan challenged Franklin about his portrayal, and when Franklin stated that it was the prerogative of the press to attack the prime minister, Callaghan replied 'Yes, I know, but every day?' The original of this cartoon was given to David Steel.

23 January 1978
Stanley Franklin
Sun

THE TUC THEN ... AND NOW

Between October 1978 and February 1979 Britain experienced a wave of industrial action on a scale that had not been seen since the 1926 General Strike. First Ford workers, then lorry drivers, council workers and NHS staff all walked out causing severe disruption to public services. This series of events came to be known as the 'Winter of Discontent' and directly led to Labour's general election defeat in May. David Low had originally created the 'honest but simple-minded' carthorse to represent the trade unions.

12 January 1979
Nicholas Garland
Daily Telegraph

BOADICEA THATCHER: DEATH BY A THOUSAND CUTS

Margaret Thatcher became Britain's first female prime minister when she won a majority at the 1979 general election. The incoming Conservative government raised interest rates sharply and brought in tough spending curbs as Thatcher claimed there was no alternative but to reduce public spending. This drew an outcry from the Labour Opposition and the trade unions, as well as some Conservatives. By 1981, she had become Britain's most unpopular prime minister since the Second World War, with seventy per cent of voters dissatisfied with her.

14 March 1981
Keith Waite
Daily Mirror

after the famous ZEC cartoon

THE PRICE OF SOVEREIGNTY HAS INCREASED – OFFICIAL

During the Falklands War, Gibbard reworked Zec's controversial wartime
cartoon (page 84) to comment upon the sinking of the *General Belgrano*.
This version also caused controversy and was cited as evidence, by the Prime
Minister Margaret Thatcher, that the British media did not support military
action. The *Sun* even accused Gibbard and the *Guardian* of treason.

6 May 1982
Les Gibbard
Guardian

10 July 1982
Kal (Kevin Kallaugher)
The Economist

Arthur Scargill was elected president of the National Union of Mineworkers in December 1981. The following year, sixty-one per cent of miners voted not to strike over pay and pit closures despite a campaign by Scargill for strike action. He repeatedly warned miners that the National Coal Board had a secret hit list of approximately seventy pits marked down for closure. He would go on to lead the miners in a year-long strike – the longest ever in the UK – from March 1984, when the closure of twenty pits was announced.

This cartoon was published at a time when paramilitary violence showed no sign of abating. In July two IRA bombs in London had killed eight people and injured over fifty others, and on 27 October three Royal Ulster Constabulary officers were killed in a massive explosion in Lurgan, County Armagh. Jak used anti-Irish stereotypes to depict the Irish as a race of psychopathic monsters who delight in violence and bloodshed. As a result of complaints made by many people in Britain and Ireland, the Greater London Council, under its leader Ken Livingstone, withdrew its advertising from the *Evening Standard* and demanded a full apology, which was refused.

29 October 1982
Jak
Evening Standard

At the Geneva Summit, President Ronald Reagan told Soviet President Mikhail Gorbachev that he would not stop work on the development of an American space-based missile defence programme. In March 1983, Reagan had proposed the creation of the Strategic Defense Initiative (SDI), nicknamed 'Star Wars', intended to defend the United States from attack from Soviet intercontinental ballistic missiles by intercepting them at various phases of their flight. Although work was begun on the SDI, much of the research was cancelled by later administrations.

6 December 1985
Peter Clarke
Guardian

This cartoon appeared the day after Margaret Thatcher resigned as prime minister. Geoffrey Howe's devastating resignation speech had sparked off a leadership challenge from Michael Heseltine, and although Thatcher defeated him in the first round, she did not win the required majority. When her Cabinet then refused to back her in a second round of leadership elections, she resigned. Heseltine publicly called for a pause in the leadership campaign to contemplate Thatcher's achievements. Chancellor John Major and Foreign Secretary Douglas Hurd announced they would stand against Heseltine in the next stage of the contest.

22 November 1990
Steve Bell
Guardian

'THERE'S THIS REALLY SCARY SCENE INVOLVING A HUGE AND HIDEOUS BUDGET DEFICIT.'

The tabloids were mostly hostile to Labour during the general election campaign, but none was as violently anti-Labour, and particularly anti-Kinnock, as the *Sun*, the country's most widely read paper. Gaskill repeats John Major's warning of a 'nightmare on Kinnock Street' from the previous day's paper with a film poster based on *A Nightmare on Elm Street*. On 8 April, the day before polling, the *Sun* ran eight pages attacking Labour under the banner headline 'Nightmare on Kinnock Street'.

1 April 1992
Dave Gaskill
Sun

Although Labour had been ahead of the Tories in the polls for some time, John Major pulled off a surprise victory in the general election. However, Tory Party Chairman Chris Patten, seen here in the bin, lost his Bath seat. The cartoonist depicted Major as a 'crap Superman', wearing his underpants over his trousers. According to Bell, 'I was looking for something that would capture his personality, and I thought of Superman. From there, it was just a matter of subverting a symbol of strength into a universal mark of uselessness.' Major's response to the underpants was that 'it is intended to destabilise me and so I ignore it'.

11 April 1992
Steve Bell
Guardian

10 December 1996
Dave Brown
Independent

John Major warned Tory Eurosceptics that attempts to hold him to ransom over Europe might imperil his chance of re-election. However, it was a price many Eurosceptics seemed happy to pay to be rid of Major. Having won the confidence vote over his handling of the Maastricht Treaty, the prime minister had just described three Eurosceptic Cabinet colleagues as 'bastards' in comments accidentally recorded after a television interview.

ELECTION 97

892·4·2·97 .

~©Steve Bell 1997~

John Major's government trailed Labour in the opinion polls and faced oblivion in the coming spring general election. According to the cartoonist: 'Major's majority slowly disappeared until eventually it was time to face the electorate once more. This time he faced a Labour Party led by its own swivel-eyed psychopath, hungry for power and even more right-wing than he was.'

4 February 1997
Steve Bell
Guardian

127

Margaret Thatcher proved an inspiration to Tony Blair, who had studied her electoral success with immense interest. He had, along with other modernisers of the New Labour project, sought to learn lessons from her dominance of the political landscape in the wake of her third general election triumph in 1987. In May Labour won its greatest ever number of seats in a landslide victory, ending eighteen years of Conservative rule.

16 March 1997
Chris Riddell
Observer

Relations between Tony Blair and Gordon Brown became strained after a biography of Brown, then Chancellor, stated he still wanted to be Labour leader. This culminated in accusations of Brown being 'psychologically flawed' by Blair's press secretary Alastair Campbell. Despite appearances, both Brown and Blair continued to resent each other. On 6 January the engagement of Prince Edward to Sophie Rhys-Jones had been announced.

10 January 1999
Chris Riddell
Observer

4 July 1999
Trog
Sunday Telegraph

Despite Tony Blair's protestations that a permanent peace deal in Northern Ireland was within reach, talks stalled over the issue of the decommissioning of weapons by the IRA. Blair's possible over-optimism is compared to Neville Chamberlain's falsely optimistic claim, after his meeting with Hitler in Munich in 1938, that he had achieved 'peace for our time'.

Addressing a conference of venture capitalists, Tony Blair departed from his script to say that people in the public sector were incapable of change. Unfortunately the speech came across as a blanket criticism of all five million public-sector workers. John Prescott, due to deliver a tough modernise-or-die message to the Local Government Association the following day, felt betrayed. He responded, without consulting Blair, by rewriting his speech to defend the public services.

9 July 1999
Peter Brookes
The Times

In the month following the opening of the Millennium Dome, it was revealed that there had been only 344,620 visitors, three per cent of the original yearly target. The Dome's management then admitted it would not meet the ten million visitor target, leading to a demand for more funding to stay afloat. They asked for a further cash injection, on top of the £110 million given in two previous loans, to cover the cost of disappointing attendances. A 2000 National Audit Office report declared that the visitor numbers had been grossly over-estimated, and that the construction of the Dome had been mismanaged.

30 January 2000
Trog
Sunday Telegraph

George W. Bush arrived in Madrid on his first official visit to Europe since becoming president. It was this event that gave the cartoonist the idea to depict Bush as a monkey: 'I started off by watching the way he walks. He holds his shoulders up and tries to make himself look taller than he is, and it makes him look like a chimp. The other thing he does is pout – he shoves his mouth forward just like a monkey does and his eyes are very close together . . . I watched his arrival in Spain . . . as he descended the steps from *Air Force One*, I knew that Bush the monkey was here to stay.' Prior to his election, apart from a few excursions into Mexico, Bush had only been abroad twice.

13 June 2001
Steve Bell
Guardian

15 September 2001
Kal
The Economist

The day after 9/11, thousands of Americans stood in front of Buckingham Palace to mourn those who had died in the terrorist attack on their homeland. For the first time, the Queen allowed the Band of the Coldstream Guards to play 'The Star-Spangled Banner', the national anthem of the United States, during the Changing of the Guard ceremony in tribute to all those who had died. Standing beyond the palace railings, many in the crowd sang along while others wept, before observing a two-minute silence.

President Bush, describing the 9/11 attacks as 'a national tragedy', also resolved that 'terrorism against our nation will not stand'. Tony Blair, for his part, stated: 'This is not a battle between the United States of America and terrorism, but between the free and democratic world and terrorism. We therefore, here in Britain, stand shoulder to shoulder with our American friends in this hour of tragedy. And we, like them, will not rest until this evil is driven from our world.' Blair had lent President Bush a bust of Winston Churchill by the sculptor Jacob Epstein.

18 September 2001
Steve Bell
Guardian

This cartoon is an allusion to Goya's *Saturn Devouring His Son*, in order to comment on Israel's treatment of the Palestinians. Many Jewish people believed the imagery was comparable to the cartoons published in the virulent anti-semitic Nazi organ *Der Stürmer*. They thought Brown was intentionally making reference to the medieval blood libel whereby Jews had been falsely accused of slitting the throats of Christian children in order to use their blood to butter their matzo. This was, of course, not Brown's intention but, primarily due to its contentious subject matter, the cartoon received world-wide condemnation. This was compounded by the embarrassing and unintended coincidence of it being published in the *Independent* on Holocaust Memorial Day.

27 January 2003
Dave Brown
Independent

People took to the streets of London to voice their opposition to military action against Iraq. It was the UK's biggest ever demonstration with at least one million taking part, although organisers put the figure closer to two million. Tony Blair, like Nelson before him, turned a blind eye to the demonstrations and warned of 'bloody consequences' if Saddam Hussein was not deposed. Horatio Nelson is supposed to have held up his telescope to his blind eye in order to wilfully disobey a signal to withdraw during the Battle of the Nile.

13 February 2003
Patrick Blower
Evening Standard

8 June 2003
Peter Schrank
Independent on Sunday

The defining issue of Tony Blair's premiership was the question of whether he misled Parliament and the British people over the threat from Saddam Hussein's weapons of mass destruction, in order to justify the invasion of Iraq. In front of the Hutton Inquiry, Blair's press secretary Alastair Campbell had been accused of 'sexing up' the government's 2002 dossier on Iraq's weapons.

Despite Tony Blair's keenness to join the euro, Gordon Brown ruled out Britain's entry into the single currency. Blair had said that staying out of it for political reasons, if the economic circumstances for entry were right, would be a 'betrayal' of Britain's national interest.

9 June 2003
Ingram Pinn
Financial Times

At the White House both Tony Blair and George W. Bush delivered a defence of their invasion of Iraq. Despite the continuing violence and the acknowledgement of major misjudgements in the execution of the war, both men still insisted that the election of a constitutional government in Baghdad had justified their decision to go to war three years earlier. Although the military campaign against Saddam Hussein was concluded quickly, bringing peace to Iraq proved to be far more difficult.

28 May 2006
Peter Schrank
Independent on Sunday

A political crisis began in Zimbabwe when inflation hit a new record high and Opposition leader Morgan Tsvangirai was beaten and tortured. This prompted widespread domestic and international criticism of Robert Mugabe. Foreign Office minister David Triesman said that Zimbabwe's government had committed 'actions . . . bordering on crimes against humanity'.

17 March 2007
Kal
The Economist

14 October 2007
Scott Clissold
Sunday Express

Gordon Brown became prime minister in June following Tony Blair's resignation. Brown's initially high poll ratings slumped when he decided against an early autumn election. The Tories nicknamed him 'Bottler Brown' and, in the Commons, Conservative leader David Cameron challenged the prime minister to 'Find a bit of bottle, get in your car, go down to Buckingham Palace and call that election.'

A first-term Democratic senator from Illinois, Barack Obama was elected
forty-fourth president of the United States, removing the last racial barrier
in American politics. His election amounted to a repudiation of a historical-
ly unpopular Republican president and his economic and foreign policies.
According to the cartoonist, 'A new dawn arose in the USA. The dark clouds
of Bushdom evaporated. This was the first cartoon I drew for the *Sun*. I drew,
gratuitously, a pair of naked breasts in the celebratory crowd as a nod to the
publication's rich history.'

6 November 2008
Andy Davey
Sun

2 March 2009
Morten Morland
The Times

Desperately needing a lift in the polls, Gordon Brown became the first European leader to visit Barack Obama in the White House. This provided the prime minister with a much-needed PR boost. 'Brown looked like the cat with the cream', observed Sir Christopher Meyer, former British ambassador to Washington. However, the British press reported that the president was 'too tired' to host the prime minister properly because he was dealing with the economic crisis.

The collapse of Lehman Brothers in September 2008 precipitated a worldwide financial crisis, which by 2009 had developed into a serious global economic downturn. The Bank of England's Monetary Policy Committee announced in March – the same week as the Cheltenham Festival – that it would begin to inject unprecedented levels of money directly into the economy, the process known as quantitative easing.

10 March 2009
Andy Davey
Sun

The Conservatives put out a poster featuring a large touched-up image of David Cameron, which gave Bell the idea to portray him with a condom over his head. As the cartoonist explains: 'The Tories' first election billboard appeared, with Cameron's supposedly airbrushed face looming large on the left. But I knew, having inspected him at close quarters, that he really was that smooth. He was going to cut the deficit, not the NHS. Total moral opportunism combined with a complete, engorged and erectile sense of his own responsibility. Thus it was that the condom unrolled over his smooth head. It seemed so perfect and so apt, to me at least, and so after some initial opposition, I elected to run with it.'

12 January 2010
Steve Bell
Guardian

The cartoonist constantly associated David Cameron with his education at Eton, and portrayed the deputy prime minister, Nick Clegg, as Cleggers, Cameron's Etonian fag. According to Brookes, 'Clegg is very much the junior partner, while Cameron has that air of entitlement about him. So, the idea of Cameron as a prefect and Clegg as his fag seemed a theme that is infinitely playable. I've called him "Cleggers" because it's a public-school way of addressing somebody.'

13 May 2010
Peter Brookes
The Times

8 March 2011
Peter Brookes
The Times

Pressure mounted on Prince Andrew over his role as trade envoy for Britain amid claims that he had become 'a national embarrassment'. This came following further revelations about his controversial dealings with discredited business figures. Downing Street had become alarmed by the prince's links with Jeffrey Epstein, a billionaire US financier who served a prison sentence for soliciting an underage girl for prostitution. Some years later, the FBI reopened its investigation and re-arrested Epstein on further charges involving underage girls.

BEST ACTOR IN A SUPPORTING ROLE

Despite Syria's bloody sixteen-month civil war, Vladimir Putin remained a staunch supporter of Bashar al-Assad. Since the beginning of the Syrian conflict, Russia had provided invaluable diplomatic support to the Assad regime, casting vetoes time after time to prevent the adoption of UN resolutions aimed at removing Assad from power.

25 February 2012
Ingram Pinn
Financial Times

149

Margaret Thatcher died at the age of eighty-seven. David Cameron, George Osborne and Ed Miliband are seen grieving by her grave. The cartoon is based on an illustration by Gustave Doré of Farinata in Dante's *Inferno*, and a reference to the closure of coal mines after the miners' strike of 1984–5. The day after publication, the *Daily Mail* castigated Bell for his disrespect under the headline 'Crawling out of the woodwork, the old Lefties spewing bile about Lady Thatcher'.

9 April 2013
Steve Bell
Guardian

As many as three Tory MPs threatened to follow Douglas Carswell and defect to Nigel Farage's UKIP unless David Cameron took a tougher stance with the European Union. Cameron had stated that he wanted to renegotiate the UK's relationship with the EU before giving people the 'simple choice' between staying in under those new terms or leaving the EU. Nigel Farage had called for firearms laws to be relaxed, calling the current ban on handguns 'ludicrous'.

13 January 2014
Morten Morland
The Times

THE LAST 'WHO WANTS TO BE A MILLIONAIRE?'

What are Labour's chances of convincing voters on the economy?

◆ A: Zero ◆ B: Zilch

◆ C: 0% ◆ D: Sod all

5 February 2014
Peter Brookes
The Times

An Ipsos MORI poll revealed that more people trusted David Cameron than Ed Miliband on the economy and unemployment. The cartoonist believed that Miliband's resemblance to the hapless Wallace damaged his chances of ever becoming prime minister.

Ed Miliband stepped down as Labour leader after his party's failure at the general election. He defended his decision to carve his party's six election pledges in stone, insisting he wanted to show the public they would not expire on 8 May. The eight-foot stone had already prompted its own hashtag, #EdStone, and was widely mocked, with critics dubbing it a 'policy cenotaph' and 'the heaviest suicide note in history'.

9 May 2015
Peter Brookes
The Times

10 May 2015
Peter Schrank
Independent on Sunday

David Cameron returned to Downing Street having won the general election. The Tories defied opinion polls by securing a twelve-seat majority in the House of Commons. Labour was decimated in Scotland by the SNP, with Nicola Sturgeon's party seizing fifty-six of the nation's fifty-nine seats. UKIP's Nigel Farage failed to win his own seat, though his party amassed millions of votes in England.

European Union foreign ministers were set to meet to discuss the continent's escalating migrant crisis, after the father of a Syrian toddler found dead on a beach spoke of how his son 'slipped through my hands' as the boat sank. The heart-breaking image of three-year-old Aylan Kurdi lying dead in the surf put pressure on political leaders to address Europe's worst refugee crisis since the Second World War.

4 September 2015
Peter Brookes
The Times

David Cameron outlined his terms for reforming the UK's membership of the EU prior to the promised in/out referendum, confident he would get what he wanted; however, the European Commission said the UK's benefits proposals could break laws on the free movement of workers. German Chancellor Angela Merkel warned Cameron she would not tolerate such an incursion into the principle.

15 November 2015
Peter Schrank
Independent on Sunday

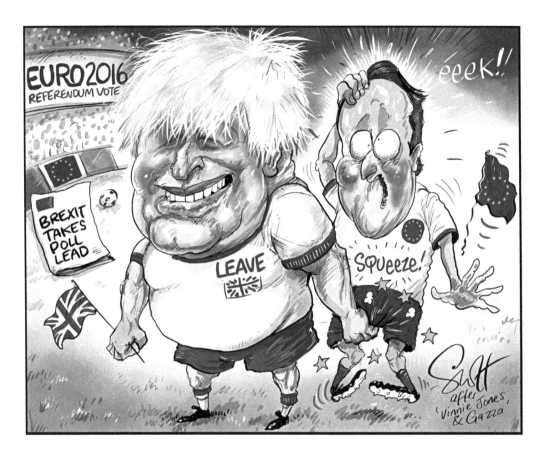

Four polls put the 'Leave' campaign ahead of 'Remain', and at this stage Leave were undoubtedly the favourites to win the EU referendum. Scott Clissold references one of the most iconic photos in sporting history, when Vinnie Jones grabbed Paul Gascoigne's crotch during a match between Wimbledon and Newcastle in 1988.

12 June 2016
Scott Clissold
Sunday Express

After a lengthy and bad-tempered referendum campaign, Britain voted to end the country's forty-three-year membership of the EU, sending shockwaves across Europe and triggering turmoil in financial markets across the globe. Senior pro-Brexit politicians attempted to distance themselves from some of the promises they had made during the campaign. Labour MP Yvette Cooper said the conduct of Boris Johnson and Michael Gove had been 'utterly shameful', and accused them of deliberately lying to voters.

25 June 2016
Ben Jennings
i newspaper

Michael Gove's betrayal of Boris Johnson was understood to be the reason for his failure to make the final round of the Tory leadership contest. Colleagues of the former justice secretary were infuriated by his unexpected decision to withdraw his backing for the former London mayor, causing Johnson to pull out of the race. Gove dropped out of the race himself after winning the support of just forty-six MPs.

8 July 2016
Peter Brookes
The Times

In his report on the Iraq War, Sir John Chilcot bitterly criticised Tony Blair for taking Britain to war. He said the notorious dossier Blair had had put together did not support his claim that Iraq had a growing programme of chemical and biological weapons. The report also condemned the Labour government for failing to anticipate the war's disastrous consequences, including the deaths of 'at least 150,000 Iraqis, most of them civilians' and 'more than a million people displaced'. The cartoon was refused publication because the implication is that Blair should take his own life. Another factor was that following Jo Cox's murder, editors were uncomfortable with revolvers as metaphors.

8 July 2016
Steve Bell
Guardian
(unpublished)

Jeremy Corbyn celebrated victory in his second Labour leadership election. New members now heavily outnumbered long-standing ones in the party's ranks, after the membership trebled to 550,000. Established party members had been more in favour of Owen Smith as leader. The surge in membership clearly demonstrated a shift to the left. After the election, 'How to leave the Labour Party' was the most searched for party-related term on Google.

25 September 2016
Scott Clissold
Sunday Express

29 March 2017
Dave Brown
Independent

Theresa May signed the letter that formally began Britain's departure from the European Union. In a statement in the Commons, she told MPs: 'It is my fierce determination to get the right deal for every single person in this country. For, as we face the opportunities ahead of us on this momentous journey, our shared values, interests and ambitions can – and must – bring us together.'

SUMMER HOLIDAY

Having lost her parliamentary majority, Theresa May hoped for some peace and quiet on a three-week walking holiday in the Alps. However, there was talk of David Davis and Boris Johnson, among others, sharpening their knives in advance of a possible leadership bid. This led some Tory MPs to advise May to introduce stronger discipline to the feuding Cabinet.

23 July 2017
Ingram Pinn
Financial Times

24 July 2017
Andy Davey
Daily Telegraph

Theresa May agreed a £1 billion deal with the Democratic Unionist Party for a 'confidence and supply' agreement. She had previously come under fire for telling nurses 'there is no magic money tree' to increase their pay, yet the deal with the DUP to cobble together a government involved this bribe money, which critics observed meant there was a magic money tree after all.

Donald Trump faced criticism from both Republicans and Democrats for his response to violence at a Virginia white supremacist rally. Hundreds of white nationalists converged to protest against the removal of a statue of a general who had fought for the pro-slavery Confederacy during the US Civil War. The far-right demonstrators, who included neo-Nazis and Ku Klux Klan members, clashed with counter-protesters. A woman was killed and nineteen people were injured when a car ploughed into a crowd in Charlottesville. Trump condemned violence by 'many sides' but stopped short of explicitly condemning the far right.

14 August 2017
Ben Jennings
Guardian

RENDEZVOUS

11 March 2018
Morten Morland
The Times

Donald Trump tweeted that a deal with North Korea was 'very much in the making', a day after revealing he had agreed to meet its leader Kim Jong Un. No sitting US president had ever met a North Korean leader. Trump had previously labelled Kim 'Little Rocket Man' and in private with aides said he was 'a crazy guy'. Kim, in retaliation, had called Trump a 'mentally deranged US dotard', a word suggesting senility. This image recreates David Low's iconic cartoon (page 69).

A RUSH OF WIND

Home Secretary Amber Rudd resigned, having come under fire after telling MPs she didn't know about Home Office deportation targets, whereas in fact she had received a memo on the policy. After accepting Rudd's resignation, Theresa May appointed as home secretary Sajid Javid, the minister for communities and local government. Javid, the son of migrants from Pakistan, said he was 'angry' about the immigration scandal and that he would do 'whatever it takes' to make it right.

29 April 2018
Nicola Jennings
Guardian

13 July 2018
Christian Adams
Evening Standard

Donald Trump criticised Theresa May's Brexit plan. He said that her attempt to forge a new 'free-trade area' with Europe would 'wreck' Brexit, stating, 'I would have done it much differently.' He also said it would 'probably kill' any trade deal with the United States. Activists planned their protests for Trump's visit to the UK with a crowd-funded giant blimp costing £29,000 that depicted Trump as a nappy-clad baby.

FIREFIGHTING EFFORTS FAILING...

Jeremy Corbyn acknowledged the existence of 'pockets' of antisemitism within the Labour Party, saying he was 'sincerely sorry' to the Jewish community. The Opposition leader said his party would 'not tolerate any form of antisemitism that exists in and around our movement'. But Corbyn's critics pointed out that many of those accused of antisemitism were vocal supporters of the party leadership.

6 August 2018
Dave Simonds
Observer

Boris Johnson announced that he had split from his wife of twenty-five years, the lawyer Marina Wheeler. Their marriage was marred by continuing claims of Johnson's infidelities; despite having four children with Wheeler, he had fathered a child with arts consultant Helen Macintyre in 2009. Johnson and Wheeler announced their divorce amid rumours that Johnson was poised to make a bid to replace Theresa May as prime minister, following heavy criticism of her Brexit policy.

8 September 2018
Peter Brookes
The Times

Ex-UKIP leader Nigel Farage launched his new Brexit Party saying he wanted a 'democratic revolution' in UK politics and that Theresa May's expected European elections were the party's 'first step'; but its 'first task' was to 'change politics'. 'I did say that if I ever had to come back into the political fray, next time it would be no more Mr Nice Guy and I mean it.'

19 April 2019
Morten Morland
The Times

171

Following intense pressure from her own government and party, Theresa May announced her resignation as prime minister. In an emotional speech outside 10 Downing Street, she outlined plans to stand down as Conservative leader in June, and said it was a matter of 'deep regret' that she had been unable to deliver Brexit. In the wake of her speech, a number of May's sternest critics including Boris Johnson, Dominic Raab, Andrea Leadsom and Michael Gove praised her for her 'duty' and 'dignity'.

26 May 2019
Morten Morland
The Times

Ahead of his visit to Britain, Donald Trump declared that Boris Johnson was his choice for the Conservative Party leadership: 'I actually have studied it very hard. I know the different players. But I think Boris would do a very good job. I think he would be excellent. I like him.'

2 June 2019
Andy Davey
Sunday Telegraph

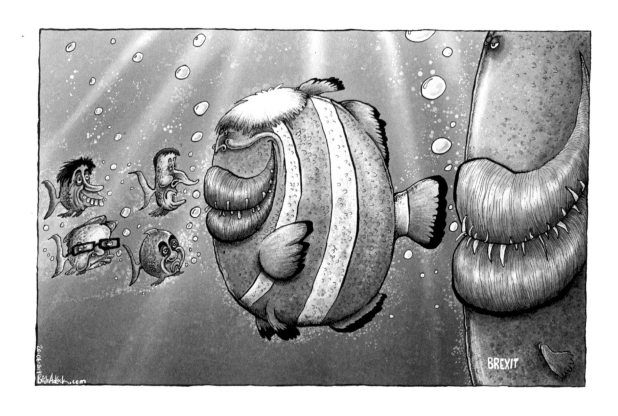

Tory MPs voted in the third round of the leadership contest. Dominic Raab, who had already been knocked out, backed leadership front-runner Boris Johnson, stating that he was 'the most credible to get us out of the EU by the end of October' and was 'absolutely committed' to meeting that deadline. 'Above all he's got the optimism. This country needs to feel good about itself and I think he's the man to deliver that.'

20 June 2019
Brian Adcock
Independent

Boris Johnson refuted lying to the Queen over the suspension of Parliament. The denial came from the prime minister in the wake of a ruling from the Court of Session in Edinburgh about his decision to prorogue the legislature. After a cross-party legal challenge was launched by opponents of the suspension, the court ruled that the advice given by ministers to the Queen over the shutdown was unlawful. Johnson maintained he had not lied.

13 September 2019
Dave Brown
Independent

BOILING POINT

Donald Trump lashed out at Democrats, calling the impeachment process, launched by US Speaker Nancy Pelosi, the 'greatest hoax', and accusing the whistle-blower and internal leakers of being spies. He also tweeted he was the victim of 'a COUP intended to take away the Power of the People'. Trump went on to call House Intelligence Committee Chairman Adam Schiff 'shifty' Schiff and a 'low-life'. He accused him of 'treason', while endorsing a claim that his removal could spark a second civil war.

4 October 2019
Ingram Pinn
Financial Times

Unionists in Northern Ireland felt a deep sense of betrayal after Boris Johnson signed a deal with the European Union which ignored red lines set out by the influential Democratic Unionist Party, rejecting a separate Brexit arrangement for Northern Ireland from that of the rest of the United Kingdom. Arlene Foster had earlier warned Johnson that her party, with its ten MPs, would oppose any deal that split Northern Ireland from the rest of the UK.

18 October 2019
Ian Knox
Belfast Telegraph

THE RED WALL...

Published two days before the 2019 general election, this cartoon correctly predicted that Labour's 'red wall' across the Midlands and the north of England, the bedrock of the party's support for generations, would crumble. The Conservatives would carve a path from Greater Manchester to Lincolnshire, the Black Country to Northumberland, as Labour strongholds fell. Some of these seats had not had a Tory MP for decades, and in the case of Burnley it had been more than a century.

10 December 2019
Morten Morland
The Times

Britain was about to leave the EU on 31 January and enter an eleven-month transition period. According to journalist Trevor Kavanagh: 'The free market clipper SS *Great Britain* is about to set sail, its hull scraped clean of bureaucratic EU barnacles. At least that's how envious Berliners see us.' He then rather prophetically goes on to say that 'China's secretive and draconian handling of the deadly "snake" virus does not encourage optimism.'

27 January 2020
Steve Bright
Sun

179

After a two-week trial in the Senate which did not call any witnesses, Donald Trump was acquitted by the Republican-dominated House of Representatives of charges of abuse of power and obstruction of Congress. When describing the Department of Justice inquiry into whether his 2016 election campaign had colluded with the Kremlin, Trump said, 'It was all bullshit . . . This should never happen to another president ever.'

7 February 2020
Dave Brown
Independent

Donald Trump 'tore into' Boris Johnson after the UK announced it would permit Chinese firm Huawei access to its 5G networks, thereby rejecting long-standing US security concerns. Trump characterised Johnson's move as a national security threat. Meanwhile, the number of confirmed cases of coronavirus in the UK doubled as the government announced new powers to detain people suspected of having the virus.

10 February 2020
Nicola Jennings
Guardian

A ninety-nine-year-old war veteran walked a hundred laps of his garden to raise upwards of £20 million for the NHS. Captain Tom Moore originally aimed to raise just £1,000 for NHS Charities Together by completing the laps before his hundredth birthday; however, he smashed his target after nearly 800,000 people made donations to his fundraising page. Tributes and messages of congratulation poured in from politicians, celebrities and NHS workers, while a petition for him to receive a knighthood was signed by more than 300,000 people. Boris Johnson said he would 'certainly be looking at ways to recognise' him.

16 February 2020
Scott Clissold
Sunday Express

BALANCING THE BUDGET

Chancellor Rishi Sunak unveiled a £30 billion package to boost the economy and get the country through the coronavirus outbreak. He suspended business rates for many firms in England, extended sick pay and boosted NHS funding. In his first Budget speech, he warned of a 'significant' but temporary disruption to the UK economy, vowing: 'We will get through this together.'

13 March 2020
Ingram Pinn
Financial Times

6 April 2020
Christian Adams
Evening Standard

Keir Starmer named his first Shadow Cabinet after his overwhelming victory in the Labour leadership contest. Claiming to showcase the breadth, depth and talents of the Labour Party, Starmer said: 'This is a new team that will be relentlessly focused on acting in the national interest to respond to the coronavirus pandemic and rebuilding Labour'.

ORANGE PHOTO-OPPORTUNITY LEADING THE WHITE PEOPLE AFTER DELACROIX

Donald Trump threatened to deploy the military if states and cities failed to quell the demonstrations and violent protests sparked by the police killing of George Floyd. The Right Reverend Mariann Budde, bishop of the Episcopal Diocese of Washington, said she was outraged after police officers used tear gas to disperse peaceful protesters from her churchyard so that Trump could stage a photo op outside. The president had walked from the White House to the church and, holding aloft a Bible, had said: 'We have the greatest country in the world. We're going to keep it safe.' The bishop's reaction was that the president had 'used the church as the backdrop and the Bible as a prop in ways that I found to be deeply offensive'.

3 June 2020
Steve Bell
Guardian

Joe Biden was elected the forty-sixth president of the United States, achieving a decades-long political ambition and denying Donald Trump a second term after a deeply divisive presidency defined by an uncontrolled pandemic, economic turmoil and social unrest. Trump, meanwhile, falsely claimed that he had won the election and vowed to move forwards with a legal fight while making unfounded claims of voter fraud.

8 November 2020
Peter Schrank
Sunday Times

Boris Johnson announced that he and European Commission President Ursula von der Leyen had reached an agreement over post-Brexit trade and security that would come into force when the UK left the EU trading bloc on 31 December. There would be no charges on each other's goods when crossing borders, and no limits to the volume which could be traded. Johnson said it was the 'biggest deal yet' and meant the UK had 'taken back control'. Ursula von der Leyen commented that competition rules designed to prevent one side gaining an unfair advantage would 'be fair and remain so'.

31 December 2020
Kal
The Economist

On 6 January, a mob of Trump supporters stormed the Capitol to stop Congress from certifying Joe Biden's election victory. Trump had urged protesters to march on the building after making false claims of electoral fraud. Both chambers of Congress were forced into recess as clashes with police ensued and tear gas was released. Jake Angeli became one of the most recognisable participants of the Capitol riots and was pictured shirtless, with a painted face and horns; he also wore a fur hat and carried a spear wrapped in the American flag. He was pictured sitting in the Speaker's chair in the Senate chamber.

7 January 2021
Christian Adams
Evening Standard

Over four million people in the UK had received their first dose of a Covid-19 vaccine as part of the largest immunisation programme in British history. The NHS vaccinated a total of 4.06 million people between 8 December and 17 January, including more than half of those aged eighty and above, and elderly care-home residents. This was more than double the number of jabs, per person per day, than any European country.

19 January 2021
Brian Adcock
Independent

Nicola Sturgeon said she would hold an advisory referendum on independence if her Scottish National Party were to win a majority in May's Holyrood elections, regardless of whether or not Westminster consented to the move. Her party set out an eleven-point roadmap for taking forward another vote. Sturgeon stated that 'the polls now show that a majority of people in Scotland want independence. If the SNP win the Scottish election in a few months' time on proposition of giving the people that choice, then what democrat could rightly stand in the way of that?'

27 January 2021
Ingram Pinn
Financial Times

The EU announces that British-Swedish drug firm AstraZeneca will now supply an additional nine million Covid-19 vaccine doses, after days of criticism of the bloc's vaccination programme. The EU was angry that Britain had received contracted supplies from AstraZeneca while it had suffered a shortfall after continuing supply problems. The EU Commission was also condemned over its threat to put checks on the Northern Ireland border to prevent vaccines produced in the EU from reaching the UK.

1 February 2021
Patrick Blower
Daily Telegraph

28 May 2021
Dave Brown
Independent

Boris Johnson and Matt Hancock defended themselves following extraordinary criticisms levelled at them by former adviser Dominic Cummings. Hancock said the 'unsubstantiated' attacks on him were 'not true'. Cummings had accused him of lying repeatedly and being disastrously incompetent as Secretary of State for Health and Social Care, and claimed he should have been fired on multiple occasions during the course of the pandemic. Johnson, who also faced claims that he was unfit for office, denied Cummings' assertion that government failings had resulted in tens of thousands of unnecessary deaths.